WHAT CHRISTIANS
BELIEVE

UNDERSTANDING THE NICENE CREED

BISHOP ROBERT BARRON

Foreword by Matthew Levering

WORD *on* FIRE.

Published by Word on Fire, Elk Grove Village, IL 60007

Cover design by Lily Fitzgibbons and Rozann Lee, typesetting by
Clark Kenyon, and interior art direction by Rozann Lee

Adapted from *Light from Light: A Theological Reflection on the Nicene Creed*,
published 2021 by Word on Fire Academic

ISBN: 978-1-68578-247-4

Library of Congress Control Number: 2024944707

The Nicene-Constantinopolitan Creed

I believe in one God, the Father almighty, maker of heaven and earth, of all things visible and invisible.

I believe in one Lord Jesus Christ, the Only Begotten Son of God, born of the Father before all ages. God from God, Light from Light, true God from true God, begotten, not made, consubstantial with the Father; through him all things were made. For us men and for our salvation he came down from heaven, and by the Holy Spirit was incarnate of the Virgin Mary, and became man.

For our sake he was crucified under Pontius Pilate, he suffered death and was buried, and rose again on the third day in accordance with the Scriptures. He ascended into heaven and is seated at the right hand of the Father. He will come again in glory to judge the living and the dead and his kingdom will have no end.

I believe in the Holy Spirit, the Lord, the giver of life, who proceeds from the Father and the Son, who with the Father and the Son is adored and glorified, who has spoken through the prophets.

I believe in one, holy, catholic, and apostolic Church. I confess one Baptism for the forgiveness of sins and I look forward to the resurrection of the dead and the life of the world to come. Amen.

Contents

Foreword

Matthew Levering

James N. Jr. and Mary D. Perry Chair of Theology,
Mundelein Seminary

I well remember the day that Robert Barron, then rector
of a booming Mundelein Seminary of the Archdiocese of
Chicago, was appointed auxiliary bishop in Los Angeles.
It was a bittersweet day, since Barron is a Chicago priest
through and through. Yet Barron has always been a great
communicator, and Hollywood, the beating heart of LA,
is about communicating great stories. In recent movies, of course, the greatest minds generally are scientists
writing equations on chalkboards regarding the splitting
of the atom (*Oppenheimer*) or striving to figure out the
whole truth of the cosmos (*The Theory of Everything*).

Barron in LA broke the Hollywood mold, even while
his presence there was also quite fitting. Here was a great
communicator, a great mind, but doing something far
beyond math and physics, unlike the scientists glorified
by recent Hollywood movies. Barron is a man of radical
God-wonder. He is thinking constantly about the wonder of a God who is not a competitor with creatures because not in any way creaturely—radically transcendent
and therefore perfectly present to each and every creature. When conversing with Barron, before you know it
you are talking about the problem of evil or about the
meaning of divine immutability.

The Nicene Creed, in Barron's vision, provides the
true "script" of the universe's drama, grounded as it is in

God and Jesus of Nazareth. In the Nicene Creed, we discover the intense excitement of God-wonder. Here is the deeper "theory of everything." But today, this story is no longer well known. As Barron says, in our present culture "the overwhelming majority of the critics of Christianity do not have a firm grasp of what thoughtful Christians actually believe."[1] They chalk it all up to irrational faith. Barron explores Christianity in this powerful book, guided by the Nicene Creed. As he knows, many people have bought into the false story that God's existence would make them smaller; God would take all the oxygen in the room and restrict their flourishing. But the Christian understanding of God is the very opposite. Indeed, the "intelligible form and intelligent purpose" that scientists rely upon when they study the atom, the cosmos, and the Big Bang are the fruit of the Creator who joyfully and graciously bestows, rather than competes with, the being and integrity of the world. In commenting on the Creed in this book, Barron demonstrates that the radical contingency of the world—its spatial, temporal, and existential finitude (which pertain to its proper beauty)—requires a transcendent Creator.

It turns out that this God is not only wondrously real but also loving almost beyond belief, with a love that possesses no self-centered neediness. As Barron says, "In giving rise to the world, God manifests the purest kind of love." But this God is also able to do something that no god would ever want to do: become man, a particular man, Jesus of Nazareth, the Messiah of God's people Israel. The Incarnation stands as the great *shock* of the

1. Robert Barron, *Light from Light: A Theological Reflection on the Nicene Creed* (Park Ridge, IL: Word on Fire Academic, 2021), xiii.

Nicene Creed. It is shocking but also fitting. Pouring himself out in love in creating, God pours himself out in love in restoring his fallen creation. In Jesus, God unites himself with his suffering creatures in order, as the long-awaited King of his people Israel, to lead the whole world to God. God can do this because he is not a being among beings; the Incarnation is not an amalgamation of two beings. Barron remarks, "The radicality of [Christ's] program of love is grounded in his Father's manner of being—which is to say, God's indiscriminate pouring forth of love." In Christ Jesus, God reveals his nature: love in a gloriously Triune form. Whereas we might want a superhero god, as in Hollywood movies, the true God comes by the path of self-sacrificial charity. This is the path of his inaugurated kingdom, the Church: the path of the Nicene Creed that we follow unto death—and unto Life.

In the present book, adapted from *Light from Light: A Theological Reflection on the Nicene Creed*, Barron communicates this breathtaking story with sure-footed intellectual seriousness, breadth, and range. But let me draw attention to the move that took place in between the publication of the original and adapted editions of this book. Serendipitously, Barron moved from LA to become the bishop of the Diocese of Winona-Rochester in Minnesota. It happens that Rochester is the home of the greatest medical facility in the world, the Mayo Clinic, to which tens of thousands stream each year in search of healing. Just as Hollywood is the heart of American storytelling, so the Mayo Clinic is the heart of American doctoring. Hollywood is not enough; its heroes of natural science and its caped superheroes cannot reach to the truth about the Creator and Redeemer. Nor is the Mayo

Clinic enough, since physical healing is ultimately not what we most need. America and the world need truth and healing. As the Nicene Creed professes, we need the revelation and healing brought by God in Jesus Christ.

The book that you hold in your hands is not the work of a mere intellectual, though it is the work of a great mind and a great communicator. This book is also the work of a soul-doctor. That makes all the difference.

I Believe

I believe

THERE IS AN ELOQUENT AMBIGUITY in the way in which the opening word of the Nicene Creed has come down to us. Our best evidence suggests that in the formula that goes back to the Nicene Fathers themselves, the word is *pisteuomen* (we believe), but as the Creed has been passed on, translated, and used in liturgical settings, *pisteuomen* often became *pisteuo* (I believe). The ancient Latin translation indeed begins with *Credo* (I believe). For the first several decades of my life, the Church commenced the Creed at Mass with "we believe," but about ten years ago, it switched back to a rendering of the standard Latin version: "I believe." I say that the ambiguity is eloquent, for there is value in both forms.

On the one hand, "we believe" effectively emphasizes the communal and corporate dimension of the Church's faith: we are in this Christian project together and never individualistically. Moreover, it indicates how, in a sense, we believe not only *with* others but in some cases *for* others. Perhaps my conviction regarding an article of the Creed is wavering, but yours is strong, and mine is firm with respect to another article, and yours is weak. The "we believe" allows us to find mutual support in our faith.

However, the "we believe" also allows us to escape, at

least to some degree, personal responsibility. Do *I* truly believe this? What is at stake in agreeing to this ancient statement is not a triviality or even a matter of purely epistemic interest. Rather, the issues raised by the Creed have to do with where a person stands most fundamentally. And therefore, in another sense, it is altogether appropriate that the one who recites the Creed commence by saying unequivocally, "I believe."

The verb itself is of crucial importance: "believe." Especially mindful of the army of the unaffiliated, those who have either never been exposed to a serious presentation of the faith or have actively left religious practice behind, I want to stress, as strongly as I possibly can, that authentic faith or belief has not a thing to do with naïve credulity or accepting claims on the basis of no evidence. Faith, in a word, is never below reason, never infra-rational. The Church has absolutely no interest in encouraging superstition or intellectual irresponsibility. Rather, real faith is supra-rational, above what reason can grasp. If we must speak of a certain darkness in regard to the matters of faith, it is the darkness that comes from too much light, rather than from defect of light.

If I might propose a somewhat homely analogy, the play between reason and faith in regard to God is something like the play between reason and faith in regard to coming to know another human being. To be sure, investigation, examination, research, and observation all play a role in this process, but finally, if one wishes to know the heart of another person, he has to wait until that other *reveals* himself, and then he has to decide whether he *believes* what he has been told. An aggressive reason that seeks always to grasp on its own terms will never come to know deeper dimensions of reality, including and especially the personal. Such depths can be plumbed only through something like a faith that accepts and receives.

It is worth noting that in Thomas Aquinas' religious epistemology, faith is a rare case of the will commanding the intellect. Typically, in Aquinas' account, it is just the opposite: will is a function of the intellect, responding to what the intellect presents to it. But when it comes to faith, the will, in a way, comes first, for it commands the intellect to assent, and it does so out of love. Because the will loves God, it directs the mind to accept what God has revealed about himself, even though the mind cannot clearly see or understand it. Again, lest this sound anomalous, much the same dynamic obtains in an interpersonal relationship. Is she telling me the truth about what is in her heart? I cannot possibly know directly, but my will, which loves her and has come to trust her, commands my intellect to assent.

"Faith" is tantamount to a willingness to attend to a voice that transcends one's own, a trusting surrender that there is a reasonability on the far side of reason. It is, therefore, an openness to adventure.

In one God

Having examined the term "believe," we must attend to the little word "in," which actually carries a good deal of spiritual significance: "*Credo in unum Deum*" (I believe in one God). In Latin, *in* with the accusative case has the sense of motion toward, while *in* with the ablative case, *in urbe* (in the city) for example, has the sense of location. Our believing does not place us firmly and certainly in the space of God; rather, it moves us toward him, into him. St. Bonaventure's searching and seminal text *The Soul's Journey into God* has a similar connotation: it is an account of how we make our way into or toward the mystery of God. This clues us into a very important dimension of creedal language. We ought never to think that acceptance of the truth of the propositions contained in the Creed is tantamount to Christian experience in its totality. On the contrary, creedal formulas are guides, guardrails, indicators on the side of the road that is leading us into God. They point us in the right direction and prevent us from going completely off the path. So, for example, if you do not believe in the Trinitarian God or in the Incarnation of the Logos or in the activity of the Holy Spirit, you are certainly in dangerous territory, and you will not tell the Christian story correctly. But the "content" of these great mysteries is not fully given in the formulas themselves; we approach that completeness only through repeated narrating of the tale and through the concrete living of the Christian life.

So, what is this "thing" that is the principal object of the act of faith? Perhaps the most basic observation we could make is that it (he) is not really a thing at all. Whatever we mean by the word "God," we do not intend one finite reality among many, not the "supreme being" in any conventional sense of that term. We intend that which brought (and brings) the whole of finite reality into being, that which transcends even as it remains intimately close to all that can possibly be seen or measured. I have found that many skeptical questions concerning God are generated by this fundamental misunderstanding of the meaning of the word. Or to state it more positively, many dilemmas and conundrums are cleared up the moment a person comes to grasp what serious Christians mean by "God." But even if we accept the correct definition of the word, is there any rational warrant for believing in the existence of this peculiar reality?

The Catholic Church has long maintained that the existence of God can be known through the light of natural reason. There is indeed biblical warrant for this: "The heavens are telling the glory of God" (Ps. 19:1), and "his eternal power and divine nature, invisible though they are, have been understood and seen through the things he has made" (Rom. 1:20). And some of our greatest theologians and philosophers have formulated arguments for the existence of God, most famously St. Anselm and St. Thomas Aquinas. Furthermore, the First Vatican Council (1869) clearly teaches that God's existence can be known with certitude through the exercise of our rational faculties. The best of our tradition has known that this knowledge has nothing to do with controlling God or with reducing him to an easily understood object of the mind. Thomas Aquinas speaks, for instance, not of "proofs" for God, but rather of *viae* or "paths" to God, and of *manuductiones*, "leadings by the hand," by which a mind is brought toward a consideration of God's existence. No one of our great masters ever taught that these "demonstrations" provide anything like an exhaustive or adequate account of God. But they do, nevertheless, point us in the right direction—and that is no small thing.

The principal challenge to religious belief is coming, today, from a materialist and secularist ideology that often claims the warrant of the physical sciences. This is the view that reality is simply coterminous with the realm of changeable matter. So, clearly on these grounds, belief in God is ruled out of court as fantastic. As a first response, we might observe that this sort of ideological materialism is self-refuting, for the claim that reality is reducible to the material cannot be justified on purely material grounds. One cannot determine through the scientific method that the scientific method is the only way to access reality. Nonetheless, many people, especially the young, are beguiled by the undoubted success of the physical sciences into accepting a "scientistic" epistemology and worldview. Therefore, in approaching the question of God today, it might be wise to seek points of overlap and connection between a religious and scientific worldview.

One argument that emerges from the world of science is that which commences from the mystical fact of the universe's radical intelligibility. Every science is predicated finally on the supposition that the world that the scientist goes out to meet through her senses and her curious, critical intelligence is marked by form, pattern, and understandability. Whether we are talking about the practitioners of psychology, biology, chemistry, astrophysics, or geology, every scientist must assume objective intelligibility. The medieval philosophers expressed this idea with typical pith: *ens est scibile* (being is knowable).

They also held that there exists so deep a correlation between the searching mind and the intelligible object that, when they meet, each, as it were, actualizes the other. Each finds its purpose in the other, something like the two halves of the mythic figures from Plato's story of human origins in the *Symposium*. Contemporary scientists implicitly affirm this truth at every turn, as they use the most sophisticated mathematics to describe dynamics of reality at all levels. They speak indeed of the "laws" or at least the statistical probabilities that govern the biological and astronomical orders, but they also assume that even the most basic levels of being, invisible to the naked eye and accessible only through indirect indications, are governed by something like mathematical principles. In the words of Cambridge particle physicist and Anglican priest John Polkinghorne, "It is an actual technique of discovery in fundamental physics to seek theories that are expressed in terms of equations that possess the unmistakable character of mathematical beauty. . . . It is something that the mathematicians can recognize and agree about."

But why should this be the case? Though we take this principle (again, unprovable through the method that thoroughly presupposes it) utterly for granted, the more we stare at it, the stranger it seems. Why should the world, in every nook and cranny and as a totality, be marked by intelligibility? Why should the scientific enterprise be undertaken with such confidence? Furthermore, why should its findings inform such remarkably successful practical projects? I have continually been amazed at the number of atheist and agnostic commentators who are content simply to accept this astonishing state of affairs as dumbly given, just the way things are. But Paul Davies challenged his scientific peers with a simple but penetrating question: Where do the laws of nature come from? And Einstein himself once quipped, "The most incomprehensible thing about the universe is that it is comprehensible."

In his indispensable *Introduction to Christianity,*

Joseph Ratzinger (Pope Benedict XVI) argued that the only finally satisfying explanation for objective intelligibility is something like a great intelligence that embedded these sophisticated patterns into the structure of the universe. Ratzinger observes how our language reflects this intuition: we speak of *recognition* of truths—which is to say, re-cognition, thinking again what has already been thought. And here we can make appeal to the Bible. One of the most important and fundamental claims of the opening chapter of the book of Genesis is that God made the universe through great acts of speech: "Then God said, 'Let there be light'; and there was light" (Gen. 1:3). "And God said, 'Let the waters under the sky be gathered together into one place, and let the dry land appear.' And it was so" (Gen. 1:9). We must not, of course, take these as literal descriptions, but rather as symbolic gestures in the direction of the intelligence that informs the act of creation. In the prologue to St. John's Gospel, which consciously hearkens back to the commencement of Genesis, we hear, "In the beginning was the Word. . . . He was in the beginning with God. All things came into being through him, and without him not one thing came into being" (John 1:1–3). If everything came into existence through a word, everything is, necessarily, stamped by an intelligible form and intelligent purpose. And this is why, according to Ratzinger and a number of other commentators, it is not surprising that the modern physical sciences emerged precisely out of a culture shaped by this biblical imagination. If one believes in creation, one will readily make two assumptions necessary for the development of the sciences—namely, that the world is not God (and hence can be analyzed and experimented upon) and that the world is intelligible (and hence likely to yield results to those who examine it intelligently). What I find particularly illuminating about this observation is how it makes clear that religion is not only not the enemy of science but in fact the condition for its possibility.

There are many other arguments that point in the direction of God: the contingency of ordinary states of affairs, immediate mystical experience, the press of moral obligation, etc. Is any one of these approaches airtight, beyond question, utterly convincing? Perhaps not. But rarely, if ever, do we assent to a proposition on the basis of a single clinching argument. Typically, we do so under the influence of a congeries of arguments, intuitions, and experiences, all of which tend along the same trajectory, and this is eminently true of our assent to the proposition that God exists.

God is that which is intelligible in itself, that which exists through the power of its own essence, that which is good by its very nature. And this implies, the Creed insists, that the God in whom we believe is one. The unity of God is, of course, an elemental biblical claim: "Hear, O Israel: The LORD is our God, the LORD alone," says the great *shema* prayer in the sixth chapter of Deuteronomy, and monotheism, it is fair to say, is *the* distinctive mark of Jewish faith. The opening verses of the book of Genesis, the account of the creation of all things, mentions a whole series of finite things—sun, moon, planets, stars, animals, mountains, etc.—that in various cultures in the ancient world were worshiped as divinities. In insisting that they are creatures, the author of Genesis effectively dethrones them, placing all of them in a subordinate relation to the one God. Joseph Ratzinger has observed that the *shema* and this opening article of the Creed have in common a spiritual implication of enormous significance. To say that there is only one God or that one believes in *unum Deum* is to disempower any false claimant to ultimacy in one's life. To say that God is the only God is to say, necessarily, that no country, no political party, no human person, no movement, no ideology is of ultimate importance. It is, accordingly, to take a stand—both for and against.

But this unicity of God can be shown in a more philosophical way as well. To say that God is the unconditioned source of finite existence is to say that God exists, not through any cause that actualizes a potential within him, but purely through the power of his own essence or nature. Hence, God is fully actual, utterly realized in being—*actus purus* (pure act) in the language of Thomas Aquinas. And from this unique metaphysical manner of existing, God's unity necessarily follows, for difference is always a function of some potentiality, some form of nonexistence vis-à-vis that from which one thing is differentiated from another. A is not B in the measure that there is something in B that is not in A and vice versa.

Therefore, there cannot be two or more unconditioned realities, two or more uncaused causes of conditioned being. Now, we might entertain the objection that, according to this logic, pantheism would have to obtain, since God could not be properly differentiated from the world. If we were to say, as we must, that God is not the world, then God would seem to have some potentiality vis-à-vis the world. But this is why we have to maintain that God's otherness is a noncontrastive or noncompetitive otherness—that is to say, that God, though certainly distinct from the world, is not lacking in any perfection that the world possesses. As Robert Sokolowski puts it, God plus the world is not greater than God alone, and "after creation there are more beings but not more perfection of *esse* [being]." In point of fact, this unique manner of God's being is precisely what permits God to involve himself in the universe in a noninvasive and finally life-enhancing way. When the gods of ancient mythology enter the world, they always do so destructively, something in the worldly order giving way in order for them to appear. But there is none of this in regard to the true God, whose relationship with creation is beautifully expressed in the biblical image of the burning bush. The closer God comes to a creature, the more that creature is enhanced and rendered splendid. We will pay very special attention to this dynamic when we turn to the creedal statements on the Incarnation of the Son of God.

2

The Father

The Father almighty

THE CREED REFERS TO THE ONE GOD as "Father almighty." When it comes to the name "Father," we immediately meet with an ambiguity, for on the one hand the term seems to be referring to God as such, especially in his capacity as Creator, but we will see, in very short order, when it is used in relation to the one the Creed calls his "Only Begotten Son," it means something else altogether. Let us simply divide these two meanings and consider the first one first.

In examining the unity of God, we were looking at an attribute that belongs, if you will, *ad intra*—that is to say, to the inner reality of God. But when speaking of his Fatherhood in the first sense of the term, we are looking more *ad extra*, to the manner in which God relates to what stands outside of him. To be a father is to be one who generates or gives rise to something other. But that characterization, though true, is more than a little austere, especially in light of Jesus' own address to God as *Abba* (Father, in a very familiar sense).

A father gives rise to another, but he also cherishes the other to whom he gives rise. One of the most compelling and puzzling questions regarding creation is why God would create at all. God, in his simplicity and unity and unconditioned perfection, is utterly good. Nothing could possibly add to his glory or his joy. So then why does he bring about finite existence? The classical answer is that he does so not out of need but simply out of a desire to share his goodness and glory, in accord with the ancient principle *bonum diffusivum sui* (the good is diffusive of itself). We recall that according to Plato, the form of the good lies beyond the realm of beings, and its basic function is to give. This is why Plato compares the form of the good to the sun, that power in whose light everything else is seen. And from this follows something of tremendous moment—namely, that God creates purely as an act of love. Love is not a sentiment, but a movement of the will. In the language of Thomas Aquinas, it is to will the good of the other. Some contemporary commentators have intensified the meaning of the Thomistic definition by adding the phrase "as other" to the end of the line. To love is to break out of the gravitational pull of the ego, truly and sincerely wanting what is best for the other. This is why Jesus can say, "No one has greater love than this, to lay down one's life for one's friends" (John 15:13), implying that authentic love expects nothing in return. It is not the indirect egotism that often masquerades as love: I will be kind to you that you might be kind to me.

In giving rise to the world, God manifests the purest kind of love, since he cannot possibly benefit from the act. As one of the prefaces to the Eucharistic Prayer in the Roman rite has it, "Our praises add nothing to your greatness." God plus the world is not more perfect than God alone. Hence, the very existence of the universe is, necessarily, the consequence of an act of absolutely disinterested love. As we will see when considering the

Trinity, this creative move is not surprising, since the innermost nature of God *is* love. Creation must be construed, indeed, as an icon or external manifestation of that primordial love. As many have pointed out, this is reflected in the German term for "there is," which is *es gibt* (it gives). This reflects the profound intuition that what appears before us *is*, but does not *have* to be, and that therefore some cause ultimately gave it to us, or better, is giving it to us. The proper response in the presence of a gift is gratitude, which is why we say "thank you" when some good is presented to us that need not be there. By a metaphysically correct instinct, we acknowledge the existence of a generous giver whenever we appreciate the gratuitous existence of the contingent world.

So, God creates; he gives rise to what is other than himself; he shares his being. It is most important to distinguish between the unique act of creation, which belongs to God alone, and the various forms of making. These latter always involve the shaping of something already existing, the way that a carpenter makes a desk out of wood, or a painter makes a painting out of oils and canvas, or a river carves out a canyon. We speak casually in this context of creating, but we really mean making. But since God is one, and properly unconditioned in his being, nothing can stand apart from him for which he is not himself ontologically responsible. There can be no matter or energy or stuff with which God works, nor pre-existing context in which he operates, for otherwise this would condition and delimit him. Time, space, energy, and matter, accordingly, are all themselves creatures of God.

This is why the great tradition speaks of God's

creation of the universe *ex nihilo* (from nothing). This is no violation of the causal principle *ex nihilo nihil fit* (from nothing comes nothing), since the world does indeed come from God as a first cause. What the adage implies is that God does not make the world out of anything, nor does he project it into anything pre-existing. In his *De potentia Dei*, Thomas Aquinas states this truth in a highly paradoxical way, reminiscent of a Zen koan: that which receives the act of creation is itself being created; and the creature is a kind of relation to God with newness of being (*creatio nihil est aliud realiter quam relatio quaedam ad Deum cum novitate essendi*). Thomas carefully draws out some of the implications of this insight. First, creation cannot be construed as a type of motion or change, since there is no uncreated substrate that undergoes a reduction from potency to act. Further, it does not take place in time, since time itself, as we saw, is a creature. Hence, it is nonsensical to speak of what obtained "before" the world began or even to speak of the "moment" of creation, as though time were marching along and then creation happened at a given point in time.

What furthermore follows is that creation is not a one-off event, something that happened long ago and now is simply in the past. Given the rapport between unconditioned being and conditioned being, creation is a continual state of affairs, obtaining moment to moment. God sustains the universe the way a singer sustains a song, in the words of Herbert McCabe. Thomas Merton showed the spiritual power of this teaching, commenting that contemplative prayer is finding the place in you where you are here and now being created by God. Not only is this dynamic perpetual, but it is also unmediated, since there is quite literally nothing that stands between the creature and the Creator, no matter or energy or potentiality that mediates their relationship. Again, this is not pantheism, since finite being is radically other than unconditioned being, and the one can never be reduced to the other. However, creation metaphysics justifies Augustine's claim that, even as he remains higher than anything we can imagine, God is also closer to us than we are to ourselves.

A further implication of the doctrine of creation is that all things in the universe are connected to one another as ontological siblings, since all are coming forth from moment to moment from the same ultimate source. Though they can appear simply as separate beings, the things that make up the world are joined, as it were, through a common center. The ethical teachings of Jesus, especially regarding the love even of our enemies, are grounded finally in this metaphysical perception. Even those who seem on the surface most alienated from us are, in point of fact, our brothers and sisters, and in a sense far deeper than the merely biological or sociological. If I might highlight a moral and spiritual feature of this teaching: God's capacity to create the world out of nothing is mirrored in God's re-creation of the soul out of the nothingness of sin. As a corruption of the will, sin is, strictly speaking, a type of nonbeing. Without any initiative on our part, God can reach out and remake a lost soul, just as, without any cooperation from another, he causes the world to be.

We must also speak, in this context, of God's providence over creation. Conditioned as we are in the West by forms of deism, we tend to think of God as a distant cause, but this is entirely unbiblical. The God of biblical revelation is intensely involved in his world, presiding over it, worrying about it, directing it toward an end. And this is confirmed philosophically as well, for the infinitely intelligent and personal God can never be other than personally present to the world that he constantly maintains. God is necessarily in the world in a deeply intentional manner.

The book of Wisdom confirms this in a lyrical statement: the wisdom of God "reaches from end to end mightily, and orders all things sweetly" (see Wis. 8:1 D-R). It is worth meditating on that term "sweetly." Once again, in accord with the metaphysics of the burning bush, God's causal influence is not manipulative, interventionary, or extrinsic to the effect, for God, as we saw, cannot be construed as one competing cause among many. God draws creation to himself nonviolently, allowing the creature under the divine influence to become itself most fully. In regard to nonrational creation, this is exercised through the intelligibility that God places within the world, which permits things to unfold according to their intrinsic meaning.

Perhaps the most vexing theological issue of all—indeed, what some consider the neuralgic point from which all of theology develops—is the question of evil, of why wickedness and suffering exist in a universe that the infinitely good God has made and that he continually directs. In providing a response to this objection, the great tradition has made a few indispensable moves. The first—which constituted a major discovery for the young Augustine—is that evil is not a positive force opposing the good, but rather a sheer negativity, a privation of being, the lack of a good that ought to be present. It is crucial to grasp that one can think of good apart from evil, but not vice versa, for to consider evil is, necessarily, to consider the good that it corrupts or compromises. And this implies that God never "creates" or "produces" evil; it cannot be ascribed to him as to a cause, and it in no sense stands against God as an ontological rival. We should speak not of God causing evil but of God's permission of evil within the confines of his creation. One might see the presence of the serpent in the garden in the book of Genesis as a poetic expression of this principle.

But still the question remains: Why would God do such a thing? Why would God permit the evil that assuredly plagues the world on a massive scale? The standard answer is that God does so in order to bring about some greater good, which could not have been accomplished otherwise. Even a superficial examination of our own experience reveals that there is something to this way of thinking. Without the painful and invasive surgery, the health of a person's body would never have been restored; without failing in one area of life, success in another might never have occurred; without the excoriating speech from a coach or teacher, one might never have realized his full potential; etc.

That God permits evil "to bring about a greater good" is a legitimate response, but as to the details of that relationship, how precisely this particular evil conduces to a particular good or set of goods, we cannot possibly say; one would have to see every conceivable implication and consequence and circumstance, stretching out indefinitely into the future, and no finite subject could ever claim such all-embracing consciousness. However, our incapacity to respond to that more exacting question should not tell against the divine providence; it should awaken in us a certain humility before the purposes of God.

Maker of heaven and earth, of all things visible and invisible

The Creed specifies that God is the Creator of both "heaven and earth." On the one hand, this is simply ancient code for "everything"—that is to say, all finite existence. Both what is above and what is below is a creature of God. To state this in more precise metaphysical language: whatever is finite and contingent in its manner of being must be traced to the unconditioned as to a first cause. This principle obtains whether we are talking about the things and people in our ordinary experience (the earth) or the highest and most rarified elements within the universe (heaven). Sometimes atheists suggest that the multiverse theory, the proposal that there are, in fact, a variety of separate universes, somehow militates against belief in God, but this is silly. Let us suppose there is an infinite number of "universes." If they are finite and contingent, then they depend, ultimately, upon the one reality that is not finite and contingent.

In the Bible, "heaven" refers sometimes to the literal sky and those things in the sky, but it also designates a realm that belongs in a unique way to God and is hence to be differentiated from "earth," which belongs more peculiarly to us. In later theology, "heaven" in this sense is appreciated as the place where the angels and saints dwell. The next phrase in the Creed might help us understand this better: "of all things visible and invisible." Heidegger recovered the primordial understanding of truth as visibility or coming into the light. Undoubtedly, the rational faculty is ordered, first, to what is at hand, to what visibly shows up: the phenomenal world of practical activity, nature, and human interaction. Following Aristotle, Thomas Aquinas states that all knowledge begins in the senses—and makes thereby much the same point. God creates this visible, more immediately obvious realm. But as Plato and his numberless disciples over the centuries have reminded us, there is a dimension of being that is not visible yet is eminently real, indeed, more real than the visible dimension. The purpose of Plato's parable of the cave is to show how the philosopher escapes from the realm of mere fleeting appearance and comes to a more substantial, though invisible, world of pure forms. One might think, also along Platonic lines, of mathematical objects and pure numbers, which are undoubtedly real but invisible, though visible representations of them can be contrived. The point that the Creed insists upon is that these realities, too, are creatures of God, despite their more elevated, less ephemeral, ontological status. We might say that they participate in the divine being in a more intense way, or perhaps, that they share in and mirror certain aspects of God's existence that material creatures do not.

Under this rubric of the invisible created realm, we must speak also of angels. The existence of angels is consistently affirmed by Sacred Scripture, both Old Testament and New, most notably by Jesus himself—and the reality of spiritual powers is confirmed across the centuries and across the cultures. Giving full weight to a legitimate skepticism regarding these claims, it still seems that only an exaggerated and ideological materialism would dismiss them simply out of hand. And following the prompts of certain theologians, both classical and contemporary, we might offer some justification for this belief. Both Thomas Aquinas in the Middle Ages and Teilhard de Chardin in the twentieth century made the observation that it would be anomalous were there simply to yawn a great ontological abyss between the wildly diverse world of physical reality—from quarks to galaxies—and the being of God. Would it not make more sense, both theologians suggest, that in between the realm of pure matter and pure actuality there would be a dimension of reality, perhaps as richly diverse as the material world, but made up of spiritual creatures? And would not it make sense, as the Bible clearly indicates, that this collection of spiritual creatures would serve a properly mediating function, acting as messengers (*angeloi*) between heaven and earth?

And this brings us to a final observation—namely, that creation, in its staggering diversity, both material and nonmaterial, serves as an iconic representation of God's existence. In his simplicity, God contains the fullness of the power of existence, and he requires the multiplicity of creation to represent that fullness, creatures emerging, we might say, as the variety of colors emerge from a prism upon which pure white light is shining. The astonishing variety on display in every corner of the created world is God's attempt to manifest the intensity of his perfection in a finite mode.

Though God does not exist in a creaturely way, every conditioned thing tells of God in its own absolutely distinctive manner. Plato famously wrestled with a troubling implication of his theory of forms—namely, whether there are forms of ordinary and crass things, such as mud and hair. A Christian theology of creation would have no problem seeing even the most ordinary creaturely realities as bodying forth an aspect of the divine perfection.

3

The Son

I. THE SON OF GOD

I believe in one Lord Jesus Christ

WITH THIS ASSERTION OF THE CREED, we come to the heart of the matter, for all of distinctively Christian faith begins and ends with a particular person, Jesus from Nazareth, recognized to be the Son of God. One might argue that practically everything I have said to this point, including the reflections on the nature of belief, the existence of God, creation, and providence, could be affirmed by devout Jews and Muslims, and perhaps even by many religiously unaffiliated. But when we come to Jesus, we arrive at a watershed, a point of demarcation. The Nicene Creed implicitly acknowledges this distinctiveness, since the section regarding Jesus is, by far, the longest in this ancient statement of faith.

The name "Jesus" (in Hebrew, *Ieshuah*), common enough in first-century Jewish culture, means "Yahweh saves." And therefore the name at the heart of Christian faith compels us to acknowledge both that God is incomparably good (for he is in the business of saving) and that something has gone wrong with God's good creation (for it *needs* saving). The book of Genesis tells us what this dysfunction is. In the compelling poetry of the opening

verses of the first book of the Bible, we find a dual assertion being made. As God speaks the world into being, we
are meant to see something like a liturgical procession.
At the end of that sacred parade comes the human being,
and the figure at the end of such a procession is always
the one who will lead the praise. Hence, we understand
the role of other creatures in relation to the human creature: the latter is to lead the former in a chorus of praise
of the Creator.

When God is given highest praise (when he is worshiped properly), then right order obtains both within
the worshiper and around her. "Glory to God in the highest and on earth peace to people of good will." Concomitantly, when something or someone less than God is
adored, disintegration follows. This is the second great
move being made in these opening verses, for everything
mentioned in the litany of creation—moon, sun, planets, animals, etc.—was, as we saw, worshiped in certain
cultures in the ancient world. By naming them as creatures, the author of Genesis is deposing them, disqualify-
ing them as objects of worship. Hence the basic formula
articulated by St. Augustine: sin is turning from God to
creatures. It is engaging in wrong praise; it is a suspension of orthodoxy (*ortho doxa*, "right praise"). In making
themselves the criterion of good and evil, Adam and Eve
turn to themselves rather than to God, and the result—
in the evocative rendering of the author of Genesis—is
an animosity among themselves, and between them and
nature. This is the fallen condition, the depth-level dysfunction, from which it is, in principle, impossible to
extricate themselves. Since the compromised will is the
problem, more human willing will not be the solution;

since the fallen mind is the problem, more human thinking will not ultimately solve anything.

Rather, some power has to come radically from without the fallen situation, but at the same time it has to enter fully into it. Though I am anticipating the fuller argument a bit, Jesus (Yahweh saves) is precisely that figure. Savior, derived from the Latin *Salvator*, the bearer of the *salus* or health, is related to the English word "salve." Jesus is, in his very person, the salving of the wound caused by false praise. The common name *Ieshuah* (Joshua in its most direct English rendering) called to mind for first-century Jews the figure of Joshua from the Old Testament, the loyal lieutenant of Moses who led the conquest of the Promised Land after the death of Moses. And this suggests another powerfully symbolic way to consider the life and work of Jesus of Nazareth. He was a warrior who set out to fight not the worldly enemies of Israel but the spiritual enemies of the human race. From the beginning of his life—even as an infant—he was violently opposed, precisely because a fallen world resists its own correction. His battle comes to a climax on the cross, and we will look in great detail at this struggle below.

The second name that the Creed gives for this Jesus is "Christ." From the Greek *Christos*, the term renders the Hebrew *Mashiach*, which means "the anointed one." Though priests and kings were anointed in the ancient Hebrew tradition, the term is used most often and with greatest resonance of David, the greatest of Israel's kings. We find in 1 Samuel the moving account of the young David being anointed by the prophet Samuel: "And the spirit of the LORD came mightily upon David" (1 Sam. 16:13). David does indeed become a priest, since he brings the ark of the covenant into his new capital Jerusalem, leading a dance while wearing the distinctive garment of a priest. He also commences the preparations for the building of the temple, which will be completed by Solomon his son. The point is that David sees the re-establishment of right praise as essential to the success of his kingdom: all the tribes of the Lord united around the worship of the one God. And David is assuredly king, indeed the greatest of Israel's leaders. His triumph was to have held off the enemies of the nation and to have expanded its borders so as to establish a kind of empire. This was, in the estimation of the ancient teachers of Israel, the mission given originally to Adam. Our first parent was meant not to remain self-satisfied in Eden, but rather to expand the borders of that paradise outward. One of the effects of the original sin is precisely a suspension, or at least compromising, of that mission. The various kings of Israel, to varying degrees, took up the Adamic task, but none realized it as fully as David.

However, what becomes eminently clear in the biblical account of King David is that, though he was to be sure a morally and spiritually imposing figure, he did not utterly fulfill his destiny. His priesthood is undermined by his frequent moral failures, most notably in connection with Uriah and Bathsheba; and his kingship is undermined by the rebellion of his son Absalom and by David's own laziness and inattention. And therefore Israel began to dream of a perfect or definitive David who would deal finally with the enemies of the nations, who would gather the scattered tribes of Israel, and who would restore right praise to the nation, and through the nation, to the world. This is the *Mashiach* whose coming

the prophets predict and whose reign the Psalms cele-
brate in anticipation.

There is probably no greater anticipation of the coming of the definitive David than in the words spoken by
the prophet Nathan to David himself (2 Sam. 7:12–17).
The Lord has promised, the prophet tells the king, that
the Lord will put a descendent of yours on the throne
forever and that his reign will last for all time. Israel
noticed soon enough that this did not have to do with
the endurance of the Davidic line in history—since that
line was broken at the Babylonian exile—but they preserved the hope nevertheless. In the opening chapter
of the Gospel of Luke, we find the account of the Annunciation. The angel Gabriel tells the Virgin Mary that,
through the power of the Holy Spirit, she will give birth
to a son and that "he will be great, and will be called the
Son of the Most High, and the Lord God will give to him
the throne of his ancestor David. He will reign over the
house of Jacob forever, and of his kingdom there will be
no end" (Luke 1:32–33). This is nothing other than the an-
nouncement of the fulfillment of Nathan's prophecy that
a definitive son of David would come, a *Mashiach par excellence*, the warrior and the priest, the Christ.

When we consult the Old Testament texts in reference to the Messiah, we encounter a fact both fascinating
and more than a little puzzling. When the Psalms and
prophets speak of the deliverer, they are referring to a
human figure, an earthly king like David, a conventional
monarch. On the other hand, they frequently refer to
God himself as the Savior of his people. In the remarkable text from Daniel 7, we see practically conflated the
figure of the Ancient of Days and a human figure, "one

like a son of man," both ruling over the world. For to this Son of Man is given "dominion and glory and kingship, that all peoples, nations, and languages should serve him" (Dan. 7:13–14).

Perhaps the best way to understand this juxtaposition is to assert that somehow Yahweh, the God of Israel, would indeed come to set things right and that he would do so through the instrumentality of a human being, the act of salvation involving both divine and human agency. What we notice in the Creed—and it can be a bit wrenching—is precisely this oscillating back and forth between language describing the inner life of the unconditioned source of existence and language describing a very particular first-century Jew. The "one Lord Jesus Christ" is this figure in his complexity. Whenever the Church wrestles with the issue of the "two natures" in Jesus—and we will consider this matter shortly—it is not engaging in purely philosophical speculation. On the contrary, it is trying to express, with at least relative adequacy, that the strange Savior, both divine and human, long anticipated throughout the Old Testament, had indeed come in the person of Jesus.

The Only Begotten Son of God

The title "Son of God" can be found in many places in the Old Testament. For example, in the book of Job, angels are referred to as "sons of God" (Job 1:6). Moreover, the Psalms make reference to the king of Israel as a "son," "begotten" of God (Ps. 2:7). Even in the New Testament, we find references to divine sonship regarding people other than Jesus himself. Thus, in 1 John we have a description of those who have the right to be "called children of God" (I John 3:1). So it appears as though "son of God" carries the sense of close rapport with God, or deep friendship with God, or familial belonging to him. Another term that is used throughout the Bible to designate those who have been entrusted with a mission is "sent." In point of fact, no one in the Scriptures is ever given an experience of God without being, at the same time, sent forth. This is true of Abraham, Jacob, Joseph, Moses, Joshua, Samuel, David, Isaiah, Jeremiah, Peter, James, John, Paul, etc.

And so Jesus is referred to clearly as the Son of God and, particularly in the Gospel of John, as the one who has been sent by the Father. For example, at his baptism, a voice is heard from heaven: "This is my Son, the Beloved, with whom I am well pleased" (Matt. 3:17). And at his trial before the Sanhedrin, Jesus is asked whether he is the Son of God, and he answers in the affirmative. Most strikingly perhaps, in Caesarea Philippi, when Jesus asks his disciples who they say that he is, Peter responds, "You are the Messiah, the Son of the living God" (Matt. 16:16). When people inquire of Jesus what they must do to be saved, he responds, "This is the work of God, that you believe in him whom he has sent" (John 6:29). At first glance, therefore, the Bible seems to be indicating that Jesus is the latest in a long line of prophets, patriarchs, messengers, and friends of God who have been entrusted with a special task on behalf of God.

But we must dig deeper. Even the most superficial analysis of the relevant New Testament texts reveals that the manner of Jesus' sonship is qualitatively different from that of anyone else named son or child of God in the Bible. For Jesus consistently speaks and acts in the very person of the God of Israel—and examples of this abound in the Gospels. Some years ago, it was a commonly accepted view that the divinity of Jesus was stressed particularly, even exclusively, in the Gospel of John and that the synoptic Gospels presented a more straightforwardly human Jesus. The "high" Christology of John was contrasted with the "low" Christology of Matthew, Mark, and Luke. But this simply is untenable. While John expresses the teaching regarding Jesus' divinity in relatively clear conceptual language—"In the beginning was the Word, and the Word was with God, and the Word was God" (John 1:1)—the synoptics equally insist on the full divinity of Jesus, though using a different kind of language and symbol system, one deeply rooted in the more poetic and allusive manner of the Old Testament. Thus, for example, in the account of the healing of the paralyzed man in the Gospel of Mark, we hear Jesus say, "Son, your sins are forgiven" (Mark 2:5). Understandably, the bystanders wonder, "Why does this fellow speak in this way? Who can forgive sins but God alone?" (Mark 2:7). The point is that Jesus had unambiguously seized the prerogative of the God of Israel. Similarly, at the commencement of the Sermon on the Mount in the Gospel of Matthew, Jesus blithely remarks, "You have heard it said, but I say . . ." (see Matt. 5:21–48). What he is referencing is the Torah, the supreme authority within Judaism, given directly by God to Moses on Mount Sinai, that to which every teacher in Israel finally appealed. By placing his own teaching above that of the Torah, Jesus is assuming the authority of God himself.

All of this proves unequivocally that Jesus' sonship and his status as the One Sent are qualitatively different than those of any other figure in the biblical tradition. Moses, Isaiah, Ezekiel, David, and Abraham might have seen themselves as servants of the God of Israel, bearers of his message, doers of his will; but none of them ever saw himself as operating in the very person of the God of Israel, doing and saying what only God could legitimately say and do. Now, as C.S. Lewis and many of his followers have pointed out, these outrageous claims on his own behalf might be construed as signs of either lunacy or moral turpitude, but Jesus' bearing and overall manner of life make these explanations completely unconvincing. However, the most powerful affirmation of Jesus' claims regarding his own person come—and we will consider this phenomenon in much more detail later—from his Resurrection from the dead, by which the one he called "Father" ratified in the most dramatic way possible Jesus' self-identification.

Therefore, when the Creed, reflecting this biblical consensus, refers to Jesus as the "Only Begotten Son of God," it is signaling this qualitative difference. It is insisting that Jesus the Son shares divinity with the Father who sent him, "Son" and "sent" in no way implying ontological inferiority to the Father and Sender.

Born of the Father before all ages. God from God, Light from Light, true God from true God

The Creed that we are considering came out of the deliberations of the Council of Nicaea in 325 and was slightly elaborated at the Council of Constantinople in 381. Therefore, at the time of the Creed's formulation, Christians had been teaching, preaching, and theologizing about the biblical witness concerning Jesus for almost three centuries. In many ways, the Nicene declaration represents a summary and distillation of that long process of reflection. Prompted by a particular challenge and operating within the conceptual framework of the time, the Nicene Creed was the Christian community's way of saying, "If you want to tell the Christian story correctly, you must follow this template."

A full analysis of the historical and theological context for the seminal Council of Nicaea would take us way too far afield, but suffice it to say that it was summoned as a response to the Christology proposed by Arius, a priest of Alexandria. Under the influence of both Greek mythological patterns of thought and the regnant Neoplatonism of his time, Arius opined that Jesus is a hybrid of a semi-human and a semi-divine nature. The "divinity" that was incarnate in him was the highest of creatures, the first emanation from the Creator, a purely spiritual Logos or Word of God, but not true God. In the famous formula that Arius and his followers propagated, "There was a time when he was not," meaning that this Logos does not possess the eternity that is the unique prerogative of the high God. Furthermore, the "humanity" in which this quasi-divine Logos resided was not a complete human nature, but rather a body controlled by the Logos, which had, as it were, supplanted the properly human soul. This is why I spoke of a mythological framework for Arius' thinking, for the hybrid of divinity and humanity that he proposes is not entirely unlike that which obtained in Achilles or Hercules, both semi-divine/semi-human figures.

Supported by Arius' own persuasive preaching, as

well as, it is said, the popular songs that he composed in its defense, this point of view gained traction, first in Alexandria and then, in time, throughout the eastern Mediterranean territories. But it also excited vigorous opposition. Various local councils were summoned to address the controversy, and finally, in 325, the Ecumenical Council of Nicaea was called by Emperor Constantine himself, eager to ensure that his newly won political unity would not be undermined by theological squabbling.

After much debate—some of it quite rancorous—the Fathers of Nicaea decided to condemn the Christology of Arius and to adopt, in consequence, a strongly anti-Arian statement. The familiar lines of the Nicene Creed, descriptive of the Son of God—"born of the Father before all ages," "God from God, Light from Light, true God from true God"—are all explicit refutations of the Arian view that the Logos incarnate in Jesus was less than the Creator God. "Born of the Father before all ages" was designed specifically to counter the rallying cry "There was a time when he was not." The peculiar phrases "God from God, Light from Light, true God from true God" were all crafted for the purpose of indicating that though this Son of God proceeds from a source (he is "from" another), that procession implies in no way an ontological inferiority vis-à-vis the source from which he comes. And these precisions are not, as some critics suggest, the result of the imposition of an alien philosophical framework on the biblical witness. Rather, they are attempts to preserve the scriptural testimony concerning the uniqueness of Jesus' sonship, using the most refined intellectual tools available at the time.

Begotten, not made

Following these evocative phrases comes a philosophical distinction of crucial importance. The Fathers of Nicaea tell us that the Son of God, incarnate in Jesus, is "begotten, not made" (in Greek, *gennetos* rather than *genetos*). In attendance at the Council of Nicaea, serving his bishop Alexander of Alexandria, was a young deacon called Athanasius. Upon the death of Alexander, not long after the conclusion of the council, Athanasius became bishop of his native city. Throughout the rest of his long life, he ardently defended the formulas of the Council of Nicaea, convinced that they constituted a standing or falling point for the Christian faith. Enduring almost constant harassment, threats of violence, and several exiles at the hands of his intellectual and political opponents, Athanasius insisted on the full divinity of Jesus. And he knew that crucial to that defense is the demarcation between *gennetos* and *genetos*.

In his masterpiece, entitled *Four Discourses Against the Arians*, the bishop of Alexandria clarified the subtle distinction between begetting and making. Both, he argued, imply the coming forth of one reality from another. But what is begotten entirely participates in that from which it comes, whereas what is made only imperfectly participates in its source. Finally, what is begotten issues, as it were, automatically from its source, while what is made comes forth through an act of the free will. Hence, the Son of God, eternally begotten of the Father, does indeed come forth from the Father, but he comes forth precisely as one who shares utterly in the being of the one from whom he comes. And he proceeds not as the product of the free choice of the Father but as a necessary accompaniment, as light comes from the sun or as wetness follows from the nature of a fountain. This is in sharp contrast to what is made by God—namely, creatures. None of these, even the highest, shares completely in the Creator's manner of being, and all of these have come not of necessity but through the choice of the Creator who was not obliged to make them. If Arius were right, the Logos incarnate in Jesus would have been, like any other creature, made. Now, lest all of this remain at the level of desperately abstract metaphysics, Athanasius shows us, in that same text, the soteriological implications of this distinction. Since God alone can save, were Jesus simply a creature, he would not be Savior. If he were made, he would require, like any other creature, the grace of God to be saved. But the consistent claim of the Church is that Jesus is not in need of salvation but is instead the source of salvation.

Athanasius' stance in the fourth century has been appreciated by some of the greatest spirits of the Christian tradition as indeed of decisive significance. It is therefore not surprising that the Church compels us, every Sunday, to rehearse Nicaea's victory over Arius. Were Arius right, Christianity would lose its soul, devolving into one more mythic or vaguely philosophical system.

Consubstantial with the Father; through him all things were made

Serving as a sort of orchestral crescendo to this line of argumentation comes perhaps the most famous and controversial word in the Nicene Creed: "consubstantial" (in Greek, *homoousios*). The Son of God, we are told, is "consubstantial with the Father." The term itself, derived from *homo* (same) and *ousia* (substance, essence, or being), was coined by Emperor Constantine's theological advisor, Hosius, who was present at the Nicene deliberations. An older English translation of the Creed rendered the word, legitimately enough, as "one in being." The most recent rendering carries the same sense: one in substance—that is, essential, underlying reality. The obvious objection, raised by some of the Nicene Fathers themselves and reiterated by theologians and philosophers in the immediate wake of the council, is that this term effectively eliminates *any* distinction between the Father and the Son, turning those designations into names of different modes of God's appearance in history. Much of the theological debate in the centuries following Nicaea circled around this eloquently ambiguous word.

This entire discussion places the Christian tradition squarely on the horns of a dilemma. On the one hand, it seems incoherent, given the unity and simplicity of God, even to speak of begettings and proceedings within the divine being; on the other hand, to speak of the Son of God as "one in being" with the Father, hence honoring the divine simplicity, seems to render impossible any sort of real play between Father and Son. One way to characterize the Christological debates that preceded and followed Nicaea is to appreciate them as an oscillation between the extreme poles of tri-theism (belief in three gods) on the one hand and modalism or Monarchianism (a rejection of the objective reality of the Trinitarian persons) on the other. When one overstresses the differentiation of the Trinitarian persons, one ends up affirming that there are three separate beings, each bearing the designation of "God." When one under-stresses the differentiation of the persons, one ends up affirming that God is one *tout court*, a "monarch" who simply displays himself according to varying "modes" of appearance.

Nicaea plays a deft both/and game, insisting that the Son of God is fully divine, "consubstantial" with the Father from whom he proceeds and, at the same time, really other than the Father, since he is "from" the Father, begotten by him. Even as the divine unity is never compromised, a real play of otherness obtains within the divine essence. Now, in the immediate wake of the Council of Nicaea, many theologians continued to struggle with the implications of its teachings. Though Arius himself died shortly after the council concluded, his point of view did not fade away; in fact, it intensified in many parts of the Christian world, both East and West, throughout the fourth century. Moreover, a compromise position also emerged, one that stood, it seemed, midway between Arianism and Nicene orthodoxy—namely, the *homoiousian* point of view. The addition of the Greek letter *iota* to *homoousios* indicated that the Logos that became incarnate in Jesus was not of the *same* substance as the Father, since this would seem to imply modalism, nor was he of a totally different substance, since that would seem to imply Arianism. Instead, he was of *similar* (*homoi*) substance to the Father. As one might expect, this compromise ultimately pleased no one, the Arians seeing it as crypto-Monarchianism and the Nicene orthodox seeing it as surreptitious Arianism.

Very much in accord with John Henry Newman's speculations about the way in which doctrine develops through the play of lively minds, the Church's under-standing of the Nicene teaching deepened and broad-ened during these controversies. In the crucible of the battle between tri-theism and modalism, a new set of terms and concepts emerged. Playing a key role in this evolution were the so-called Cappadocian Fathers: Greg-ory of Nyssa, Gregory of Nazianzus, and Basil the Great. These bishop-theologians from the eastern provinces of Asia Minor began to develop the linguistic tools that would enable Christians to affirm the *homoousios* doc-trine without falling into either problematic extreme.

Their efforts came to full fruition in the speculative theology of St. Augustine of Hippo. In his seminal *De trinitate* (*On the Trinity*), composed roughly a century af-ter Nicaea, Augustine proposed an analogy for the Trin-ity that went a long way toward resolving the dilemma bequeathed to the Church by the Nicene Creed and that, sixteen centuries later, still beguiles and illumines. Our own spiritual faculties of mind and will, Augustine ar-gued, display in their dynamics something of the unity and diversity within God. There is the *mens* (mind), the aboriginal, chthonic ground of all of the spiritual activ-ity of which a human being is capable; the capacity of this elemental mind to know itself, to pose itself as an "other" for its own contemplation, which Augustine calls *notitia sui* (knowledge of self); and finally, the abil-ity of the *mens* to will itself as something good, an act of self-possession he terms *amor sui* (love of self).

Augustine sees this spiritual dynamism as a strikingly good analogy for the Trinitarian relations within God. The "Father" is the divine *mens*, the elemental ground of God's life. The "Son" is God's *notitia sui*, his great act of self-knowledge, appropriately designated as Logos or interior Word. And the Holy Spirit is God's *amor sui*, the love shared by the Father and the Son. As is the case in regard to human psychology, the distinctions are real, but none of them involves a compromising of the unity and simplicity of the divine nature. We can at least begin to see how the Son could be "from" the Father and still be "true God from true God," how he is indeed begotten but not made.

Though this language can seem hopelessly abstract and thin, in point of fact, it puts us very concretely on holy ground. When we speak of God, we are speaking of the source and ground of all finite reality, that which is most real, the fullness of being. To remark, therefore, a play of relationality in the very heart of God is to make a metaphysical claim of extraordinary reach and power. It is to say that something like "being toward another" belongs to the very essence of God. And since God is the ground of finite being, this ordering to another is, somehow, ingredient in every aspect of the universe.

Indeed, the term used typically to designate the ontological status of the Father, Son, and Holy Spirit is "person," from the Latin *persona*, derived, in turn, from *per-sonare*, to sound through. In its original sense, *persona* indicates the mask worn by a theatrical actor, which had within it a device for the amplification of the performer's voice, so that he could "sound through" to another actor or to the audience. Something like speaking to, communicating with, belongs to the ground of reality, even before the act of creation established other beings with which or with whom God could communicate.

In light of these metaphysical clarifications, we can

begin to understand the ethical teaching of Jesus more profoundly. When Jesus urges his followers to love (to will the good of the other) in the most radical way, loving even those who hate us, even those who are our enemies, turning the other cheek when we are struck, refusing to answer evil for evil, he is moving far outside the ambit of standard ethics, either ancient or modern. He is proposing something far beyond the goodness of the ethically upright person imagined by Aristotle, Kant, or Wittgenstein. The radicality of his program of love is grounded in his Father's manner of being—which is to say, God's indiscriminate pouring forth of love, "[making] his sun rise on the evil and on the good, and [sending] rain on the righteous and the unrighteous" (Matt. 5:45). Many other religions and philosophies speak of God having the quality or attribute of love, but only Christianity makes the astonishing claim that "God *is* love." And this can be true if and only if a being toward the other marks the ownmost nature of God, even prior to creation. Therefore, G.K. Chesterton was right when he observed that the doctrine of the Trinity is simply the conceptually precise manner of saying that God is love, that there is, in the divine reality, a play of lover (the Father), beloved (the Son), and shared love (the Holy Spirit).

It is most important never to forget that, even as we climb the heights of metaphysical speculation in regard to the Trinity, the roots of this doctrine are in the very particular Jew, Jesus of Nazareth. Prophets and patriarchs spoke to God and even, in some sense, heard the voice of God. But when Jesus speaks to his Father, or when the Holy Spirit intervenes in the life of Jesus, we are not witnessing just one more human being in dialogue with his

Creator; rather, we are overhearing, as it were, a conversation taking place within the inner life of God.

II. THE SON OF MAN

For us men and for our salvation he came down from heaven

The "why" of the Incarnation is one of the most contested questions in the history of Christian theology. What we find in the New Testament, in marvelous variety, is an array of metaphors and images, each one expressing, in a unique way, the *experience* of coming into contact with Jesus, either directly or indirectly through the mediation of the Church. Though each of these symbols gave rise in time to doctrinal positions, it is a useful exercise to sense the feeling-tone that they were originally trying to convey. Jesus' death and Resurrection were like a liberation. So Paul can say, "For freedom Christ has set us free" (Gal. 5:1). It was like being ransomed from slavery—and thus Paul can speak of Christians being delivered from powers and principalities. It brought peace and joy, what biblical Jews would have called *shalom*—and therefore the word "peace" rings like a bell throughout the New Testament. It was like being set right, straightened out—and so St. Paul, again and again, could speak of the "justification" that comes from participating in the life of Jesus. And it was like receiving a completely unmerited gift—and thus almost all of the authors of the New Testament speak of "grace" in connection with the Lord.

Now, the biblical authors were not choosing their images and metaphors at random. Rather, they reached, as we would expect, to their Scriptures, which had schooled them to expect certain favors from the God of Israel. The entire Exodus narrative, which haunted the minds of practically every New Testament author, taught them to look for God's liberation and deliverance from oppression. The prophets—especially Isaiah and Jeremiah—predisposed them to expect that God would act to set things right and to establish a lasting peace. They knew from the entire drama of Israel's history that God had chosen Israel not because of its accomplishments and merits, but simply as an act of gracious love. And thus they saw all of this brought to complete and unexpected fulfillment in the life, death, and Resurrection of Jesus of Nazareth. I believe that all of the above is implied in the creedal phrase "for us men and for our salvation . . ."

If anyone is ever tempted to see the Nicene Creed as simply an abstract doctrinal catalogue, this very line should disabuse him of the notion. What is at stake in this series of propositions is *salvation—soteria* in the original Greek of the Creed, suggesting healing—not just the clarification of concepts. How wonderful that the language of the Creed turns subjective at this juncture. To this point, it has directed us outward to the truths that we believe, but here we are directly and existentially involved: "for us men and for our salvation." In a word, what we are dealing with in this Creed is the be-all and the end-all of the human endeavor. It treats of what matters most, or to use Paul Tillich's phrase, "ultimate concern."

The Creed then tells us, a bit quaintly, that the Son of God "came down from heaven." We are obviously not meant to take this language literally, as though God dwells up in the sky and has to make a physical transit to the earth. As we saw earlier, the unconditioned source of all creaturely existence cannot be located in space, since such a location would render him conditioned. Further, as purely actual, the Creator God is not a thing that can move from place to place. "Heaven" is being used here as a symbol for the transcendence of God, for his otherness to the world of conditioned objects and events. It is also evocative of God's moral manner of being, which is radically different from the world of fallen moral agents with which we are accustomed.

And thus we see the importance of saying that the Son of God "descended" from the realm of divine transcendence. If sin is a kind of dysfunction that has infected the whole of the human family—and this is indeed the best way to understand the doctrine of original sin—then the solution has to come from outside of the dysfunction. Just as someone fully in the grip of an addiction cannot lead another addict out of his misery, so someone who is completely conditioned by sin cannot save another sinner. Rather, as we saw, the Savior from sin must indeed enter into the world of sinners, but he cannot be himself a sinner. Instead, as Athanasius clearly saw, he had to "descend" from a realm not marked by cruelty, hatred, violence, and fear.

And by the Holy Spirit was incarnate of the Virgin Mary, and became man

It is a peculiarity of the Nicene Creed that the Holy Spirit is mentioned, almost in passing, before belief in him is formally professed. I will have much more to say about the third person of the Trinity in due course, but it is worth sharing at least a word about the Spirit here, particularly as he is mentioned in connection with enfleshment or incarnation.

The Holy Spirit is referenced in the very opening lines of Sacred Scripture. The author of Genesis tells us, "In the beginning when God created the heavens and the earth, the earth was a formless void and darkness covered the face of the deep, while a wind from God swept over the face of the waters" (Gen. 1:1–2). The "wind from God" is the *ruach Yahweh*, often rendered as the "spirit" of God, and his "sweeping" or "hovering" over the surface of the deep carries in the Hebrew the sense of a mother bird beating her wings over her young, encouraging them to fly. The *ruach Yahweh* is, accordingly, the creative power that will give rise to the universe in all of its complexity and its variegated physicality: waters, sky, earth, plants, trees, animals, and humans. Throughout the history of salvation, the spirit of God is what stirs the prophets to speak and empowers kings—think of the *ruach* that "came mightily upon" David when he was anointed by Samuel the prophet. Moreover, the Spirit of the Lord came down upon Jesus himself at his baptism and then "drove him out into the wilderness" (Mark 1:12). He is an active, creative force who makes things happen and compels people to move. Therefore, it is hardly surprising that the *ruach Yahweh* is intimately involved in the enfleshment of the Son of God, an event that will result in a renewal of creation.

The clear implication of the Creed is that the two principal agents in the bringing about of Jesus Christ were the Holy Spirit and the Virgin Mary, grounding the doctrinal conviction that in him two natures—divine and human—came together. And so we turn to a consideration of the Virgin Mary. The Creed's unabashed affirmation of the virginity of Mary the mother of Jesus is grounded in the biblical claim, on clear evidence in both the Gospel of Matthew and the Gospel of Luke, that Mary became pregnant without the intervention of a human father. When, in Luke's account, the angel tells Mary that she will become the mother of "the Son of the High," the young girl responds, "How can this be, since I am a virgin?" And Gabriel assures her, "The Holy Spirit will come upon you, and the power of the Most High will overshadow you; therefore, the child to be born . . . will be called Son of God" (Luke 1:34–35). In Matthew's telling, an angel appears in a dream to Joseph, Mary's betrothed, and explains how her pregnancy came about: "Joseph, son of David, do not be afraid to take Mary as your wife, for the child conceived in her is from the Holy Spirit" (Matt. 1:20).

The virginity of Mary seems fitting for a number of reasons. First, it indicates, as clearly as possible, that God is involved in the coming to be of Jesus. Though human cooperation, at both the physical and moral level, is required, the Incarnation would not have happened without a gracious divine initiative. Further, it signals that the Incarnation involves not simply a revolution in the moral and spiritual order but an entirely new creation. Just as Adam, on the biblical telling, is made through the direct causality of God, so the New Adam is made *de novo*, and not in the ordinary course. Finally, the virginity of Mary is a sign of the purity and completeness of her devotion to God, making her a fit vessel for the divine Messiah. She becomes mother in the physical order, though she is given utterly over to God; she is, as classical Christian piety would have it, spouse of the Holy Spirit. All of this, one might argue, is summed up in the greeting that the angel gives Mary at the Annunciation, the most sublime offered to any human being in the biblical tradition: *kecharitomene*, "full of grace."

Many skeptics across the ages have put the doctrine of the Virgin Birth of Jesus forward as an indisputable sign that the Church is retrograde, stuck in a pre-scientific, superstitious mindset. Is not the birth of Jesus from a virgin, they wonder, just another iteration of a mythic trope found in cultures around the world? First, as Hans Urs von Balthasar has argued, the story of the birth of Jesus from a virgin and those similar narratives from mythic traditions are only superficially similar. The more intently one studies the Gospel stories, the more unique and distinctive they appear. One clear indication: in almost all of the tales of the birth of divine children from virgin mothers, the pregnancy happens through the violent rape of the human mother by a divine father. There is none of this in the Gospel narratives. Indeed, in the courtly play between the angel of the Annunciation and the Virgin Mary, practically the opposite of rape is on display.

But the most striking difference is that the myths give themselves away by their very genre: they are, quite obviously, symbolic literature, intended to indicate natural processes or general truths about the rhythms of the seasons. But the Gospel narratives concerning the birth of Jesus are placed very purposely within a recognizable historical and geographical context, grounding them in fact: "a decree went out from Emperor Augustus . . . while

Quirinius was governor of Syria" (Luke 2:1–2). And they are a propaedeutic to what is assuredly the biography of a real, historical figure, clearly unlike the narratives concerning Horus or Mars.

But is this teaching, the critics insist, not simply repugnant to reason, even if we grant that it differs from similar accounts? That skeptical claim is grounded in the meta-assertion that the miraculous, strictly speaking, is impossible. However, once we affirm the existence of God, which, as we saw, can be done on rational grounds, this dismissal of the miraculous appears more or less arbitrary. To be sure, miracles are rare, for if they were not, we would not "wonder" at them, which is the state of mind implied in the word *mirari*. But what would prevent the creative source of all finite existence, who continually makes the world from nothing and sustains it from falling back into nonbeing, from producing a state of affairs outside of the normal course? What would be irrational about saying that God, on rare occasion and for his very particular purposes, might suspend or circumvent the natural regularities that he himself established? If God can bring something from nothing, he can surely cause a virgin to become pregnant.

Mary the Virgin also carries an extraordinarily powerful symbolic value for those with eyes to see. On the façade of Notre Dame Cathedral in Paris, there is a statue of Mary the Mother of God, and over her head is a depiction of the ark of the covenant, the holiest artifact in ancient Israel, the ceremonial container for the Ten Commandments and the rod of Aaron. The association is far from accidental, for Mary was seen as the fulfillment *par excellence* of the ark, since she herself bore the presence of God within her womb. And if we allow our symbolic and associative imaginations even wider play, we can see Mary, as the Church Fathers did, as evocative of the holy people Israel itself, who bore, over long centuries and through much suffering, the word of Yahweh. In light of these symbolic connections, Mary's words to Jesus at the wedding feast of Cana take on their full resonance: "They have no wine" (John 2:3). Here, she represents all of the patriarchs and prophets of Israel, crying to the God of Israel, "How long, O Lord? How your people yearn for the joy and salvation that only you can bring." And when she tells the waiters at the wedding, "Do whatever [Jesus] tells you" (John 2:5), she is, once again, all of the sages and seers of Israel, urging the holy people to follow the promptings of the Lord. It is from Mary's womb, and indeed from the womb of Israel, that the Messiah is born.

Having considered the two great agents of the Incarnation—Mary and the Holy Spirit—I want to look with careful attention at the extraordinary word that stands at the heart of this article and indeed of the Creed in its totality: *sarkothenta* (he became flesh). The Son of God, we are told, becomes incarnate (enfleshed) through the power of the Holy Spirit. It is crucially important to see how counterintuitive this assertion is to both the Greek and the Jewish mind. For biblical Jews, God is indeed the Creator of matter, and flesh is indeed good, but God himself is neither material nor fleshly. Jesus is operating out of a thoroughly Jewish framework when he tells the Samaritan woman at the well, "God is spirit, and those who worship him must worship in spirit and truth" (John 4:24). By the same token, those schooled in the classical philosophical tradition insisted that God is immaterial and that his nonmateriality is one of the marks of his ontological superiority. Precisely as finite, changeable, corruptible, and conditioned by both time and space, matter cannot belong to the divine manner of being.

But the Nicene Creed intimately associates the God of Israel, the Creator of the world, with matter, even to the point of speaking of his entry into flesh. What sense are we to make of this? First, we must avoid any temptation to say that the Incarnation involves God "turning into" matter, ceasing to be spiritual and becoming flesh, as though he changes from being one type of reality to another. All of that is ruled out by God's simplicity and immutability. Writing some 120 years after the Council of Nicaea, the fathers of the Council of Chalcedon insisted that the two "natures" that come together in Jesus do so "without confusion or change, without division or separation." What is divine in Christ and what is human in him do not lose their respective integrity or bleed into one another.

When Nicaea speaks of God "becoming" human, therefore, it means that God the Son took to himself a human nature—which means a fully constituted human manner of being—in order to use it as an icon of his presence and action. We recall that St. Paul, in his Letter to the Colossians, referred to Jesus as the "image of the invisible God," and the Greek term that stands behind "image" is none other than *eikon*. Those in the Eastern Christian tradition who pray in the presence of icons tell us that the sacred picture is much more than a mere representation; rather, it participates in the reality that it represents, drawing the viewer through itself to the invisible order. As became apparent to the disciples on the

Mount of Transfiguration, Jesus' humanity functioned in precisely this way, as a radiant sign through which his divinity shone. Mind you, in using this comparison, I am by no means suggesting that the Lord's humanity is a flat and purely passive vehicle by which his divinity is made manifest. On the contrary, precisely in the measure that it is a complete human nature, it involves intellect, will, and freedom. It is by means of this richly complex humanity that Jesus' divinity expresses itself.

This was, by the way, the central issue of the so-called monothelite controversy in the seventh century. Eager to affirm the full divinity of Jesus, some theologians held that there was, in the Lord, only one will—namely, the divine will—and that this source of freedom and action effectively supplanted the properly human source of freedom and action. But Maximus the Confessor and others rose to meet this challenge, convinced that monothelitism denied the principle implied at Nicaea, and confirmed a century later at the Council of Chalcedon, that the natures subsist in their integrity and without mixing or mingling. Maximus and his colleagues insisted that there are, in Jesus, two wills, divine and human, just as there are, in him, two minds, divine and human. Thus, even as we speak of the humanity of Christ as an "icon" of his divinity, we by no means imply that it is a truncated or compromised humanity. In point of fact, the very unconditioned quality of God's way of being guarantees that these two freedoms can coexist noncompetitively within the unity of Jesus' person.

Having stressed the integrity of the two natures in the Incarnation, we must now highlight the extraordinary truth that these two distinct manners of being *come together*, precisely in the unity of one divine person. Jesus is not two separate beings, nor is he a mere human person in an intimate rapport with God, in the manner of a great saint. Rather, in the unity of one person, he is both divine and human. To grasp how this is possible, we must remember what was said above about the unique nature of God. As the act of being itself (*ipsum esse*), God is not one being among many, competing for space on the same ontological grid as other beings. His otherness to the world, as we saw, is noncontrastive and noncompetitive. And this is why he is able to enter into union with a creaturely nature, without undermining his own nature or compromising the creature that he becomes. In the created order, one thing can become another only through aggression, supplanting, or surrender. Thus, the house becomes a pile of ash through being destroyed by fire; the zebra becomes the lion only by being devoured; one person "becomes" another only through domination and manipulation. But God does not relate to creaturely natures in this way. Rather, as we have seen, when God comes close to a creature, that finite thing becomes more truly itself.

Though I have followed the Creed in laying out the truths about God before expounding the truths about the Incarnation, I would hold that, in the order of discovery, things moved in the opposite direction. It was from the noncompetitiveness of the natures in Jesus that Christian theologians eventually concluded to God's strange and utterly unique quality of existence. When they mused on what God must be like if the Incarnation in fact took place, they understood that God is not a conventional supreme being but is rather best described as

Being itself or "that than which nothing greater can be thought."

It is also important to look at the famous phrase "became man" from the other side. What does it mean for humanity that God became one of us? It implies that divinization is, for all of us, a real possibility. By this, the great tradition does not mean that we are absorbed into the divine being, for that would be misreading the Incarnation along the lines suggested above, but just from the human side of the equation. Nor does it mean that any of us is capable of becoming a son of God in the way that Jesus was. But the Fathers of both Eastern and Western Christianity came together in affirming that it does imply the possibility that our lowly nature can be so elevated as to be described as participating in the Trinitarian life.

The Greek-speaking theologians referred to this, unabashedly, as divinization (*theosis* in Greek), and their Latin-speaking counterparts followed them in characterizing it as *deificatio*. This is why the goal of the Christian spiritual life is never simply moral excellence, as indispensable as that is, but rather mystical participation in the divine life. One of the most surprising but consistent affirmations of the early Church, formulated by theologians both East and West across many centuries, is *Deus fit homo ut homo fieret Deus*, which means, quite literally, "God became man that man might become God." In many ways, the distinctiveness of Christianity, in comparison to any other religion or philosophy, is contained in that line. There is, frankly, no humanism, either ancient or modern, more dramatic and thoroughgoing than orthodox Christianity, which envisions not simply moral achievement or political stability or economic advantage or psychological well-being as the goal of human life, but rather divinization.

III. THE DESCENT

For our sake he was crucified under Pontius Pilate

There are precisely three human beings mentioned in the Nicene Creed: Jesus, Mary, and Pontius Pilate. The first two, quite obviously, are intimately involved in the Incarnation, which stands at the heart of the Creed. But why would Pontius Pilatus, the early first-century Roman governor of the province of Judea, play such a prominent role in this profession of Christian faith? One very simple and yet very significant service that the mention of Pilate performs is to ground Jesus unambiguously in history. No one wonders who the local magistrate was when Hercules cleaned the Augean stables or who the ruler of Egypt was when Osiris rose from the dead. This is because those stories were and are recognized clearly as mythic in form. But in the case of Jesus, the first Christians were extremely interested in telling the world the name of the Roman authority who presided over the death of their Lord, lest one might be tempted to relegate the story they were telling to the generic realm of the mythical. The fact that there are coins, inscriptions, and documents from the period that clearly reference Pontius Pilatus confirms this instinct.

But Pilate is present in the Creed for a deeper reason. He presided over the Crucifixion and death of Jesus, and upon this awful fact Christian preaching and teaching finally depend. As Paul put it in his first letter to the church in Corinth: "When I came to you, brothers and sisters, I did not come proclaiming the mystery of God to you in lofty words or wisdom. For I decided to know nothing among you except Jesus Christ, and him crucified" (1 Cor. 2:1–2). The terrible death of Jesus was not a mere tragedy, not an unpleasant fact that we must brush aside in order to get to the ethical substance of Jesus' message; somehow, it was (and is) the very heart of the matter, the hinge upon which all of Christian faith turns. And therefore it is exceptionally important that we know why Pontius Pilate and his many colleagues and collaborators, both Roman and Jewish, brought Jesus to the cross.

I would like to put this in the widest possible context. In many ways, the entire Bible is a book of battles. I am not speaking simply of the many military conflicts narrated therein; I am speaking of the almost constant struggle between the ways and purposes of God and those forces that stand opposed to the divine intention. From the opening lines of the Scriptures, we find the Spirit of God drawing life and order from the *tohu wabohu*, the watery chaos. Even in the Garden of Eden, we find the serpent, indeed the cleverest of God's creatures, but also a source of tremendous mischief. In the wake of original sin, Adam and Eve fall into conflict with one another and with the realm of nature. Cain hates his brother and murders him. By the time of Noah, sin had become so pervasive that the *tohu wabohu* returns in the form of an all-destroying flood. Once established through a series of covenants, the holy people Israel is opposed on every front and from within.

All of this comes to full expression in the New Testament. From the very commencement of his life, Jesus, the one who speaks and acts in the very person of God, is opposed. When we read the familiar Lukan Christmas account through the right interpretive lenses, we see that it is far from a charming story that one might recite to children. Instead, it is marked, through and through, by the themes of conflict and opposition. The tale opens in the way that one might expect, by invoking great and mighty figures: Quirinius, the Roman governor of Syria, and Caesar Augustus, who effectively ruled the world. But Luke turns our expectations upside down when he makes it clear whom the narrative is about: not Caesar and Quirinius, but two obscure figures making their way to Bethlehem, prompted by Caesar's imperious call for a census of the whole world. The baby to whom the woman is about to give birth is the focus of Luke's attention.

We must read the account, in point of fact, as a contrast between two ideas of kingship. The baby is born in a cave or a stable and placed in a dirty trough where animals eat. The best protected and best fed person in the ancient world would have been Caesar, and such advantages are normally seen as perquisites of the powerful. The baby is wrapped up in swaddling clothes, rendering him utterly incapable of movement. The most mobile and rangy person in the ancient world would have been Caesar Augustus, able to accomplish practically anything he wanted, and such a capacity is normally appreciated as a mark of the good life. Caesar had an enormous army, which is why he was capable of dominating his world. But the baby king, we discover, is the commander of a *stratias* (army) of angels, and this provides the hermeneutical key to the narrative. True world-conquering power is associated with humility, love, nonviolence, and poverty, not with the qualities valued by a fallen world. The Lukan Christmas story is something like an operatic overture, since it anticipates the central theme that will mark almost every aspect of the coming drama. Two kings, two ideas of kingship, two rival conceptions of power will battle against one another throughout the Gospel, and the *point* of the story is that one of them wins out.

Though his ultimate victory is indicated by the army of angels, the new King will endure, his whole life long, the opposition of the established powers of the world, both religious and political—and behind these figures, of the dark spiritual powers that stand athwart the purposes of the Creator God. By the end of his life, Jesus had been rejected by the Jewish establishment and by many ordinary Jews, by the Roman establishment, and indeed, by his own most intimate followers. With the exception of the Apostle John, every single one of his chosen twelve abandoned, betrayed, or denied him at his moment of greatest need. What I hope is clear is that the Gospel writers emphasize the *universality* of the rejection of Jesus. It was not "the Jews" or "the Romans" who turned on him; it was sinful humanity. Full stop.

As Karl Barth frequently argued, we do not really understand the nature and destructiveness of sin until Jesus appears, for it is only in contrast with his brilliance that the darkness of the world is made fully manifest. This is why, furthermore, Barth insists that the Creed's statement that Jesus "suffered" under Pontius Pilate should be taken broadly indeed, so that the whole of Jesus' life might be seen under the rubric of suffering and opposition. Here the Protestant Barth agrees with the Catholic John Courtney Murray, who said that the Gospels recount the ever-increasing *agon* between Jesus and the world that he enters. We also recall C.S. Lewis' marvelous remark to the effect that the Son of God came on the scene so quietly and unobtrusively, in a dusty corner of the Roman Empire, since he had to sneak clandestinely behind enemy lines.

Now, all of the preceding was intended to provide the context for the claim that Jesus was crucified under Pontius Pilate. His condemnation was obviously not the result of an arbitrary whim of the Roman governor, but instead was conditioned, on the New Testament reading, by the entire history of humankind's rejection of God and the ways of God. For Søren Kierkegaard, the answer to the easy theological liberalism of his time, which blithely argued that the Incarnation corresponded to the deepest aspirations of the mind and heart, was the shock of the cross. If we are all implicitly religious, and if Jesus is the teacher who gently shows us the deepest truth about ourselves, then why did we kill him when he came? When the Truth appeared in person, all of our lies were exposed, all of our pretensions to spiritual achievement unmasked.

He suffered death

As Fleming Rutledge points out, St. Paul's statement in the first chapter of Romans to the effect that he is not ashamed of the Gospel is a peculiar remark (Rom. 1:16). Why, we wonder, would Paul have to reassure his listeners and readers that the content of his preaching is not a matter of shame? It would be difficult to imagine, say, the Buddha or Confucius or Muhammad saying something comparable about his own teaching.

The simple reason is that the central content of Paul's proclamation was a crucified criminal. We are so accustomed to seeing religious images of Jesus on the cross that much of the horror and humiliation of crucifixion is lost on us. But for a person of the first century, operating within the confines of the Roman Empire, crucifixion was about the worst thing he or she could imagine. So terrible was it in fact that Cicero, one of the most eloquent and articulate men of that age, would refer to the act of crucifixion only by means of a tortured circumlocution. For the first several centuries of the Christian era, there is, outside of a mocking graffito, no known depiction of the crucified Jesus. What was involved in that form of capital punishment was just too vividly present in the popular imagination.

The Romans, it is speculated, inherited the practice from ancient Persia, but it is fair to say that they perfected it. The condemned man was usually compelled to carry the cross beam to the place of execution, where it was fixed to an upright pole. The victim was stripped naked—the humiliation of this being part of his torture—and then fastened to the device, either by ropes or nails or perhaps both. (There is indeed archeological evidence of an ankle bone, from the first century, pierced through by an enormous nail.) He was subsequently left to die, exposed to the mocking of the crowds and to the cruelty of the elements and the wild animals. But the exquisite misery of the cross consisted in the slow asphyxiation that it produced in the one who hung thereupon. And if the victim were nailed through wrists and ankles, the constant rocking up and down in order to breathe would give rise to excruciating (*ex cruce*, literally "from the cross") agony. Depending on the age and health of the condemned, the process of dying could last hours or, in many cases, several days and nights. And when the ordeal was finally over, the body was typically left on the cross until the animals devoured it, as a very public disincentive to run afoul of the Roman authorities.

Due to its horrific nature, death by crucifixion was reserved to the worst enemies of the state and to those of lowest social status: brigands, prisoners of war, traitors, and slaves. It is instructive to note that St. Paul, in virtue of his Roman citizenship, was given the far nobler death by quick decapitation, whereas St. Peter, enjoying no such privilege, was, at least according to tradition, crucified upside down. No one should be surprised to read that, even for Jews, death in this manner was appreciated as a sign of divine disfavor: "For anyone hung on a tree is under God's curse" (Deut. 21:23). Moreover, for the first followers of Jesus, his death by crucifixion was a source not only of intense personal sadness but also of deep embarrassment, since there was, for a Jew of that time, no more evident sign that someone was not the Messiah of Israel than his violent death at the hands of the enemies of Israel. For the *Mashiach* was meant to be a new David, who would deal definitively with the nation's foes and reign as the Lord of the world. Therefore, seeing the one they took to be the Messiah writhing on this instrument of torture and death, the disciples must have thought that their commitment and proclamation had been a pathetic waste of time. The whole awful process was undoubtedly a source of shame.

And yet these same disciples went careering around the world declaring precisely this crucified man as Lord and Messiah! As N.T. Wright has frequently insisted, even from a strictly historical standpoint, the emergence of Christianity as a *messianic* movement is, to say the very least, an anomaly. They did not hide the fact of the Crucifixion; they brought it to the fore. So why did they announce a crucified Messiah, and how did they come to understand the meaning of his death? The Creed cites the death of Jesus laconically enough, but the great tradition has provided a number of templates and models for interpreting it. I will explore just two of them—namely, Jesus as victor and Jesus as sacrifice. Let us take the first one first.

If we read the artfully crafted Passion narratives in each of the four Gospels, we see that the entire array of God's enemies, the full tide of the *tohu wabohu*, swept Jesus to his cross. He was David against Goliath, a naked and defenseless young man facing the giant bearing scimitar and spear and clothed in armor. But he fought, not in the conventional manner, not meeting force with force, not answering fire with fire, but rather, in accord with his own teaching from the Sermon on the Mount, with nonviolence, turning the other cheek, saying, "Father, forgive them; for they do not know what they are doing" (Luke 23:34). It is crucially important to bear in mind that we are dealing here not simply with a heroic human being, but rather with the Son of God, the one who is "God from God, Light from Light, true God from true God." *God* is fighting those forces opposed to him, and he is doing it in a way congruent with his own nature. In sharp contrast to the speech, action, and purpose of the Son of God, the enemies of Jesus show themselves for what they are.

Properly unmasked, the very worst of the dark powers, both visible and invisible, were hurled at him, and he responded by swallowing them up in the ever greater, ever more powerful, divine mercy. The "world" is allowed to do its worst, spending itself on him, and he wears it down. His nonviolence and infinite divine forgiveness effectively undermine wickedness, giving it nothing from which it could draw further energy, absorbing all of its momentum. Thus, in a very real sense, Jesus on the cross "takes away the sin of the world" (John 1:29).

Many of the Fathers of the Church attempted to express the significance of Jesus' death through the metaphor of battle, giving rise to what came to be characterized as the *Christus Victor* theory. In one version of this scenario, the devil is pictured as a great fish and the humanity of Jesus as the bait on a hook. When the devil, enticed by the opportunity of conquering this particularly heroic man, takes the bait, he is caught on the hook, which is evocative of the hidden divinity of the Lord. A tad fanciful, but still telling. The powers of the world did indeed perceive Jesus as one man among many and did indeed try to stamp him out, but what they did not see was the capaciousness of the divine forgiveness concealed behind the icon of Jesus' humanity. In devouring him, they found their own wickedness devoured.

In another version of the *Christus Victor* scenario, the devil is imagined as a kidnapper who has absconded with the human race and holds every person tightly in his arms. Jesus appears as the perfect, untrammeled man and offers himself to the devil in exchange for his prisoners. So beguiled by the prospect of catching this supreme prize, the evil one opens his arms, releasing the entire human race, and makes to seize the Lord. At this point, Jesus reveals his hidden divinity, which is more than powerful enough to overwhelm the devil, who finds himself now utterly bereft and defeated. Again, this is a highly imaginative, even comical, picture, but it speaks a rather profound truth. Human beings are meant to belong to God and to serve his purposes. Through sin, they have effectively handed themselves over to an alien lord; they have become slaves of a ruthless taskmaster. The very purity and perfection of Jesus' humanity beguiles the forces of darkness and draws them out. In the very act of taking him, they let go of what they had held captive.

The *Christus Victor* approach helps us to see how the cross of Jesus has functioned, up and down the centuries, as a sort of taunt to the powers of the world. As we saw, for Jesus' contemporaries, there was nothing more terrifying than a Roman cross—and yet the first Christians held it up, celebrated it, proclaimed it. What was meant to be an incontrovertible sign of Roman power became the incontrovertible sign of its defeat. And so it has functioned to the present day as a warning to the avatars of sin and a beacon to those whom sin has imprisoned.

A second great template for understanding the meaning of Jesus' death is that of sacrifice. Admittedly, the idea of making a sacrifice in order to placate divine powers is, to say the least, alien to our contemporary consciousness. And the classical idea that Jesus performed on the cross a bloody sacrifice that was somehow demanded by his Father strikes many people today as, at best, incredible, and at worst, the archetype of both patriarchal oppression and child abuse. I can testify that when I was going through university and seminary studies, the notion, usually associated with St. Anselm, that Jesus' death involved a sacrificial atonement for sin was customarily dismissed.

But a fundamental problem with dismissing the Anselmian theory out of hand is that, in its basic outlines, it is grounded unambiguously in the Scriptures. In describing the contours of his mission, Jesus himself says, "The Son of Man came not to be served but to serve, and to give his life a ransom for many" (Mark 10:45). And the night before his death, in reference to the Passover bread and cup, he clearly gave a sacrificial interpretation to the cross that he would endure the following day: "This is my body, which is given for you"; and even more tellingly, "This cup that is poured out for you is the new covenant in my blood" (Luke 22:19–20). Moreover, in Ephesians, we find what is unmistakably temple talk: "Therefore be imitators of God, as beloved children, and live in love, as Christ loved us and gave himself up for us, a fragrant offering and sacrifice to God" (Eph. 5:1–2). And there are many more such passages from the New Testament that we could cite. Therefore, it is certainly facile to argue that the Anselmian theory represents simply a medieval accretion.

In order to understand this approach to the death of Jesus, it is best to commence with the biblical idea of sacrifice, the basic logic of which is actually quite straightforward. The religious devotee would take some aspect of God's creation—the first fruits of his harvest, food products, unblemished animals, etc.—and he would offer them back to God in order to indicate thanksgiving, reparation, petition, or sorrow for sins. The Bible is eminently clear—and this is backed up by good metaphysics—that the true God has no *need* of such offerings, for indeed how could the Creator of the totality of the universe ever benefit from what he himself already gave in its entirety? Nevertheless, such sacrificial gestures are for the good of the one who makes them, bringing him or her on line with God, re-establishing right relationship with the Creator. In that sense, God is "pleased" with our offerings, since his delight is in what redounds to our benefit.

In terms of the Crucifixion of Jesus, the type of sacrifice that comes to the fore is the sacrifice of expiation or reparation. When someone presented himself at the Jerusalem temple to make this sort of sacrifice, he would bring an unblemished animal—bull, sheep, goat, or dove—and would, with the assistance of the priest, slit the animal's throat while the priest caught the blood in a bowl. Then the beast would be burned, either whole (a holocaust) or partially, returning it thereby to God. The spiritual psychology behind the gesture seems to have been this: what is happening to this animal should, by rights, be happening to me. The goat or bull was, as it were, standing in for the person who offered it, representing him in a quasi-sacramental manner.

This substitutionary dynamic was on particularly clear display on the Day of Atonement, the one day in the Jewish liturgical year when the high priest was allowed to enter the Holy of Holies in the temple. He slaughtered and sacrificed a number of animals in the course of the day, but the spiritual high point was the symbolic imposition of the sins of Israel onto the scapegoat. The animal so burdened was then driven from the temple and, led by a priest, brought deep into the desert where he was abandoned to certain death. Symbolically, he thereby bore away the sins of the people, representing both their degradation and their repentance before God.

There was, even within the Old Testament, furthermore, an analogy between the animal sacrifice offered in the temple and a sin-offering sacrifice made directly by a human being, representative of the entire nation. I am referring, of course, to a series of mysterious and extraordinary texts in the fifty-second and fifty-third chapters of the book of Isaiah. The prophet envisions a time when the God of Israel would be victorious, but then he segues almost immediately into the surprising description of the one through whom that victory would be won: "He was despised and rejected by others; a man of suffering and acquainted with infirmity. . . .Surely he has borne our infirmities and carried our diseases. . . .He was wounded for our transgressions, crushed for our iniquities; upon him was the punishment that made us whole, and by his bruises we are healed" (Isa. 53:3–5). Just as the animals brought to the temple for sacrifice should be unblemished, so this suffering servant would be a man of righteousness and innocence: "The righteous one, my servant, shall make many righteous" (Isa. 53:11). In light of temple practice and these extraordinary texts, it is not difficult to see why the first Christians reached for sacrificial language when attempting to explain the significance of Jesus' terrible death.

At this point, I should like to return to St. Anselm's theory and look at it with fresh eyes. In accord with his rationalistic tendencies and under the influence of his feudalistic culture, Anselm speaks of the offended honor of God the Father and of the requirement, in strict justice, that a price be paid to restore that honor. Since the offense of sin belongs to the human race, a human being had to be involved in the payment, but since the offense to the honor of God is infinite, only God could *adequately* pay it. Therefore, the righteous anger of the Father could be quieted only by the suffering and death of someone who is both God and man. This bit of theological reasoning, which explained with admirable economy *cur Deus homo* (why God became man), was one of the great intellectual achievements of the Middle Ages. And its principal virtue is that it takes the real damage of sin—what Anselm calls the *pondus peccati* (the weight of sin)—seriously.

Why could not God simply forgive human wickedness with a wave of his hand, with a stentorian decree? Of course, as Thomas Aquinas indicates, God could have done so, but such a detached pronouncement would not have *dealt* with sin. It would not have *repaired* what needed repairing. I would urge us not to think of the restoration of the Father's honor as something taking place within the psychology of the Father, but rather something taking place in us and for us, since God's honor or glory is precisely that we be fully alive. God is "offended" by sin, not in the sense that his subjective well-being is compromised, but in the sense that he hates and wants to eliminate whatever harms his beloved creatures.

Further light might be shed on both templates if we consider the theorizing of Hans Urs von Balthasar regarding the cross of Jesus as the furthest trajectory of the Incarnation. Following the prompt provided by the famous hymn in the second chapter of Paul's Letter to the Philippians, Balthasar appreciates the Incarnation as a downward movement from equality with God to identity with the human race: "Though he was in the form of God, [Jesus] did not regard equality with God as something to be exploited, but emptied himself, taking the form of a slave, being born in human likeness" (Phil. 2:6–7).

But the descent of the Son of God did not stop with his becoming human, for "being found in human form, he humbled himself and became obedient to the point of death—even death on a cross" (Phil. 2:7–8). How wonderfully that last phrase sums up everything we said above about the horror of crucifixion. The point is that God went all the way down, as far as he could go in the direction of godforsakenness, taking on pain, sickness, psychological and spiritual distress, even the agony of total isolation from God. He thereby made all of them potentially a route of access to the Father, effectively sanctifying them. Or, if we wish to shift the metaphor, he "conquered" them, robbing them of their power permanently to separate us from God. Or, to put it in the sacrificial context, he took them on in order to take them away.

One might summarize this theology of the cross as follows. The Son of God went to the limits of alienation from God so that even as the worst sinner runs with all of her energy away from the Father, she finds herself running into the arms of the Son. Here we can see the deep soteriological implications of the Trinitarian doctrine. It is only because God can, so to speak, open himself up, become other to himself while remaining one in essence, that he can embrace all of sin, even the most thoroughgoing rebellion. This is the condition for the possibility of the victorious battle of the cross and of the efficacious sacrifice of the cross.

And was buried

After mentioning the death that Jesus suffered, the Creed adds, simply enough, "and was buried." Is there anything that signals the finality and irreversibility of death more than burial? While the wake and funeral services for a loved one are ongoing, there is still a sense that they are with us; but when the body is lowered into the grave and covered over by earth, we know that they have left us forever, that they are, as the ancient Romans put it, no longer *inter homines* (among human beings). To affirm, therefore, that Jesus was buried is to affirm that he was truly dead.

Over the centuries, there have been fanciful attempts to show that Jesus did not die on the cross but swooned, only to be revived later. That a dreadfully wounded man, staggering half-dead out of his tomb, would ever be mistaken for the risen Lord is, of course, beyond ludicrous. The Romans were skilled executioners, and if there were any doubt that the cross had done its terrible work, the lance thrust into the heart of Jesus should have eliminated it. It is interesting to note that the Gospels themselves and numerous summary statements of the Paschal Mystery throughout the New Testament make special reference to the burial of the Lord, presumably to hammer home the facticity of his death.

In his study of this article of the Creed, Balthasar speaks of the *Todsein Gottes*, literally the "being dead" of God. He means that the downward trajectory of the Incarnation reaches its limit here, in the tomb of Jesus, when the Son of God enters into the experience of having no experience, into the negation, the nonbeing, of death.

Having hit rock bottom, the Son of God finds solidarity with all those human beings who have come to that same awful place. The *Catechism of the Catholic Church* cites an ancient homily on Holy Saturday, which highlights the silence and passivity of the buried Christ: "Today a great silence reigns on earth, a great silence and a great stillness. A great silence because the King is asleep."

In this context, Balthasar makes reference to Hans Holbein's ghastly depiction of the dead Christ, in the presence of which Dostoevsky himself fell into a state of agitation, a scene reproduced in his novel *The Idiot*. Most depictions of the dead Jesus are placid and serene, the Lord appearing to be asleep, the Resurrection a sure expectation. But Holbein's picture, clearly based upon his observations of a real corpse, is horrific. The wounds of Jesus are large and discolored, his eyes are half-opened, his chin up-turned and distended, his entire body turning a sickly blue, and rigor mortis rather obviously setting in. Prince Myshkin, the main character in Dostoevsky's story, cries out upon seeing Holbein's canvas: "Why, a man's faith might be ruined by looking at that picture!" Unless and until we feel something along those lines, we probably have not come to grips with what it means to say that Christ was buried. Indeed, a superficial faith might be wrecked by coming into contact with Christ truly dead and buried, but a robust faith accepts this truth as integral to the entire event of the enfleshment of the Son of God, his identification with the whole of what it means to be human.

Though the Nicene Creed simply says "and was buried," the Apostles' Creed, after mentioning his burial, says of the dead Jesus that he "descended into hell." There are, most likely, two biblical references that stand behind this claim. The first is the assertion, expressed in numerous places in the Old Testament, that the dead go to a shadowy underworld called *Sheol*. This is not a place of heavenly refreshment or spiritual fulfillment; it is instead a dismal and dissatisfying realm where shades of human beings live a sort of half-life, cut off from community and, most painfully, the praise of God. A particularly telling description of *Sheol* can be found in Psalm 88: "I am counted among those who go down to the Pit; I am like those who have no help, like those forsaken among the dead, like the slain that lie in the grave, like those whom you remember no more, for they are cut off from your hand" (Ps. 88:4–5). Jesus' descent into hell means that he has entered into solidarity with those at the furthest possible remove from the mercy of God. Though it is odd to say, it coheres with a Trinitarian logic: God goes to those cut off from God and overcomes thereby a separation that could never be overcome from the human side.

And this brings us to the second scriptural inspiration behind the doctrine of Christ's descent into hell—namely, 1 Peter 3:18–20: "He was put to death in the flesh, but made alive in the spirit, in which also he went and made a proclamation to the spirits in prison, who in former times did not obey." The prison in question here is undoubtedly *Sheol*, and the prisoners are those dead who, in their lifetimes, had wandered from the path of God. That Jesus preached the Gospel—or better, revealed it in his very person—to these long-forgotten people is a source of tremendous consolation. How else could we possibly claim the possibility of salvation for those who had lived and died before the saving event of the

Incarnation? This passage helps us see that what happened in Jesus, since it was grounded in a properly divine subject, has a ramification across all of space and time.

IV. THE RISE

And rose again on the third day in accordance with the Scriptures

The Resurrection of Jesus Christ from the dead is the fulcrum on which all of Christian faith turns. If Jesus did not rise, everything in Christian theology, philosophy, social action, art, spirituality, and morality loses its *raison d'être*. As St. Paul put it, bluntly enough, "If Christ has not been raised, your faith is futile and you are still in your sins" (1 Cor. 15:17). Without faith in the Resurrection of Jesus, Christianity devolves, immediately, into a vague mythic system, religious philosophy, or generic spirituality.

There has been, from the beginning of Christianity, a temptation to de-mythologize the Resurrection, turning it into a symbol or cipher. But if Jesus did not truly rise, then his claims to be speaking and acting in the person of God would be invalidated; and if these are invalidated, then all talk of Incarnation is negated; and if Incarnation does not hold, then the dogma of the Trinity falls away. And if the Trinity collapses, all speech about the Holy Spirit is nugatory. And if there is no Holy Spirit, it makes no sense to refer to the Church or to its sacraments. Finally, if Christ has not been raised, then we have no reasonable hope of personal resurrection. What I have just demonstrated is that 90% of the Creed craters in upon itself if Resurrection faith disappears. So wrestling with this strange "be-all and end-all" teaching is required work for every generation of Christian believers.

To be fair, the de-literalizing tendency, found in both the ancient Gnostics and in too much of contemporary theology, is, in a way, understandable, for this proposition has always been, to put it mildly, hard to believe. It is a gross misrepresentation to argue, as some do today, that ancient people, in their prescientific naïveté, were apt to believe any wild claim. They might have been prescientific, but they were not foolish. The assertion that a dead man had come back to life and had been seen by eyewitnesses was as staggering and improbable then as now. For just one bit of evidence in this regard, consider the scoffing reaction of the sophisticated Athenian crowd when Paul proclaimed the Resurrection of Jesus, as reported in Acts 17. But as Søren Kierkegaard said, the purpose of Christian theology is to make Christianity *hard* to believe. As counterintuitive as this seems, this move is indispensable lest the faith decline into a mere echo of the culturally regnant philosophy or psychology—in other words, into something not worth believing. The *hardest* doctrine to accept—and hence the most important doctrine of all—is the Resurrection.

Following the lead of N.T. Wright and many others, I would like to get at the Resurrection through a sort of *via negativa*, delineating, first, how it should not be understood. In the ancient world, there were many views in the marketplace of ideas regarding what happened to someone after she died. We might start with the Jewish thought world. There are numerous texts in the Old Testament that regard death as simply the end, full stop. As we saw, there are other texts in the Hebrew Scriptures that indicate the existence of shadowy *Sheol*, a place of virtual nonexistence where the shades of the dead continue, in a deeply mitigated condition, to be. By the time of Jesus, a third proposition had gained a wide acceptance—namely, that the righteous dead would be raised bodily at the end of time, in a sort of general resurrection of the dead. But nothing from this matrix of Jewish reflection on the state of the dead is adequate to what the first witnesses of the Resurrection were reporting.

Certainly by the time of the New Testament, the classical Greek philosophical understanding of the survival of the soul was well known, especially in those parts of Mediterranean society under Hellenizing influence. Following the lead of Socrates and Plato, Greek thinkers opined that the soul, given its essentially immaterial nature, would survive the death of the body and go, happily enough, to a realm more agreeable to it, away from the particularity and changeability of matter. Even more influential than Plato was the great epic poet Homer, whose account of life after death profoundly shaped the thinking of both ordinary people and sophisticates: in the accounts of the afterlife state of Achilles, Patroclus, and others, the dead live in a realm not unlike the *Sheol* of the Old Testament. Within the Roman cultural context, on the more popular (and political) level, we encounter the expectation of deification (*apotheosis*) for military heroes, certain political figures, and most especially for Roman emperors. Still others within the Greco-Roman world—and to a degree, even within the Jewish context—believed in some version of metempsychosis, the return of the soul to a different incarnation. Once again, none of these frameworks apply to the New Testament accounts of Jesus' Resurrection.

So what precisely do the first Christians claim about the resurrected Jesus? Perhaps the best way to put it is this: what some Jews expected of all the righteous dead at the end of time has happened to this singular figure, Jesus of Nazareth, within time. This one man has risen, even now, *ek tōn nekrōn* (literally, "from out of the dead ones") and moved once again among us. Now, having made these remarks about the objectivity and corporeality of the Resurrection, it is singularly important to emphasize that the resurrected Jesus is not like those personages described in the New Testament—the daughter of Jairus, the son of the widow of Nain, Lazarus—who came back from death but to an absolutely ordinary existence in this world and who were destined to die again. As extraordinary as those events were, they could best be described as "resuscitations," not entirely unlike what happens to those who had near-death experiences and subsequently returned to tell the tale.

Though the risen Christ is, in one sense, the same Jesus who walked the hills of Galilee and died on a Roman cross outside Jerusalem, in another sense, he is transformed, strange, not entirely of this world. This otherness is signaled, in almost all of the accounts of his post-Resurrection appearances, by the fact that the witnesses remain confused, hesitant: "Now the eleven disciples went to Galilee, to the mountain to which Jesus had directed them. When they saw him, they worshiped him; but some doubted" (Matt. 28:16–17); "While in their joy they were disbelieving and still wondering" (Luke 24:41).

The consistency of this theme—especially in documents whose central purpose was to convince skeptics of the truth of the Resurrection—is striking and certainly reflects the vivid memories of those who encountered Jesus after the Resurrection. They were trying to take in something quite new, but that was appearing within the context of their ordinary experience. If I can borrow an idea from speculative physics, they were attempting to articulate what it was like to sense a phenomenon on an event horizon, on the borderline between two different dimensional systems. Signs of the uncanniness of the risen Jesus include his ability to pass through walls, to appear and disappear suddenly, and to know states of affairs even when he is not physically present.

Without the apparitions of the risen Jesus, Resurrection faith would never have emerged. Attempts to argue that the Resurrection is merely a symbol for inner convictions of the Apostles—for example, their feeling of being forgiven by him or their sense that his cause would go on—are simply untenable, given the extraordinary stress on the objectivity and materiality of the risen Lord.

But having said this, we must also acknowledge that the second indispensable element in the emergence of Resurrection faith is the empty tomb of Jesus. If the body of the Lord were still in the sarcophagus in the garden adjacent to Calvary, no number of appearances would have convinced a first-century Jew that Jesus had risen from the dead. They would have written those off as hallucinations or fantasies. Once again, given the normal connotation of "resurrection," an enemy of the faith would simply have to indicate the presence of the moldering body of Jesus in order to refute the claim that Jesus had risen from the dead. Proposals made by some contemporary writers that no one would have known the location of the tomb of Jesus since, like most common criminals, his body would have been hurled into a mass grave or simply devoured by wild animals, strain credulity. It is not the least unlikely that a figure as prominent and as revered as Jesus would have had a wealthy follower such as Joseph of Arimathea, who might well have provided a tomb for his Lord. And thus there is no reasonable ground for doubting the consistent Gospel assertion that the site of his burial was well known.

It is therefore of considerable interest that all four Gospels draw attention to the fact that Jesus' tomb was empty, St. John going so far as to describe the burial cloths left behind, even the manner of their disposition. To be sure, an empty tomb by itself would not have provided sufficient ground for belief in the Resurrection, for the body might easily enough have been stolen or moved. But when the fact of the empty tomb is combined with the numerous accounts of Jesus appearing alive again to his disciples, Resurrection faith finds firm ground.

Having determined, at least to a sufficient degree, the nature of the Resurrection, what is its significance? As we have hinted already, the first great implication of the Resurrection is the ratification of Jesus' daring claim to speak and act in the very person of God. Had he remained in his grave, he would have been remembered by history as at best a tragically heroic figure, but more likely, as a bit of a madman. However, having risen from his grave, he received, the first Christians were convinced, the most extraordinary confirmation possible of his identity and mission. Having seen their crucified Lord alive again, how could the disciples doubt that he was the One Sent, the unique Son of the Father? To put this in the properly Jewish context, the Resurrection was vivid proof that

Jesus was indeed the Messiah of Israel, the culmination of the story of salvation. He was the fulfillment of covenant, temple, prophecy, and Torah—all of the great institutions of Israel. As St. Paul would put it, Jesus is the "yes" to all the promises God made to his holy people (2 Cor. 1:20), though that "yes" came in a remarkably unexpected way.

Secondly, the Resurrection provided an entirely new interpretive lens for the reading of Jesus' Crucifixion. As we saw, dying on a cross was, in the old dispensation, a perfect indication of failure on the part of the victim, and victory on the part of the political establishment that passed the terrible sentence. But the rising of Jesus proved beyond doubt that the power of God is greater than the power of Caesar, greater than the power of Rome—and indeed, as we read in St. John's Gospel, "greater than all else" (John 10:29). The Messiah, the new David, was indeed victorious, but in a manner that no one envisioned. When Jesus appeared alive again to those who had betrayed, denied, and abandoned him at his moment of greatest need, he did indeed show his wounds in order to remind them of what "the world" had done to him. However, he then uttered not a word of condemnation or recrimination, but rather the word *shalom* (peace), which sums up the hope of Israel and the intention of God toward his people and toward his entire creation.

A third implication of the Resurrection is that it proclaims the kingship of Christ to the world. This kingship was declared, ironically enough, by Pontius Pilate, who over the cross placed a sign declaring in the three great languages of that time and place—Hebrew, Latin, and Greek—that the crucified Jesus was "the King of the

Jews." If Jesus had not risen from the dead, Pilate's mocking sign would have remained just one more affirmation
of Roman power; but given the Resurrection, it became
the first great act of evangelization. The term *euangelion* (glad tidings) was, in Jesus' time and place, a word
with strong political overtones. When Caesar won a victory, evangelists were sent out with the *euangelion*, the
glad tidings that Rome had triumphed. How wonderful
that the first Christians played with this term, turning
it around for their own purpose, declaring a victory not
of Caesar but of Christ. The opening line of the Gospel
of Mark, which by common scholarly consensus was
the first Gospel written, expresses this admirably: "The
beginning of the good news of Jesus Christ, the Son of
God." Given all of this, it is easy to see why the powers
that be have always trembled at a bold and realistic declaration of the Resurrection.

Fourth, the Resurrection demonstrated that the sacrifice of the cross had been accepted. As I clarified above,
this has nothing to do with the successful mollification
of a dysfunctional father's anger. Rather, it means that
the work of reparation on behalf of the entire human
race has been done. Something has been offered back to
the Father—namely, the loving obedience of the Son—
which is so pleasing to God that it effectively rights the
wrongs of the world, wiping away the debt of sin. What
appears in the Resurrection of Jesus are the fruits of that
reparation, the effects of that sacrifice. The Son of God
journeyed to the furthest extreme of alienation from
God—he made that supreme sacrifice—in order that he
might reach even the most desperate sinner and open up
a path of return. If Jesus had simply stayed in his tomb,

that path would not have opened up, and his sacrifice would have been a meaningless gesture. But when he returns from utter desolation with the divine forgiveness on his lips, he gives hope to every sinner.

Finally, the Resurrection of Jesus from the dead indicates, as dramatically as possible, that God has not given up on his creation, and that his intent is to bring all of it, even lowly matter, to a glorious state of being. Just as God created all of matter—even the humblest instantiations of it—so he intends to save all matter. Platonic salvation is indeed about the escape of the soul from the prison of the body, but biblical salvation *always* involves the body. In this context, I think of a peculiar remark of the great American Catholic writer Flannery O'Connor. In the face of rationalist critiques of the miraculous, O'Connor said that the Virgin Birth, Incarnation, and Resurrection should be seen not as one-off exceptions to the laws of nature but revelations of the true laws of nature, of nature as it is intended to be. The Resurrection of Jesus is a proleptic breakthrough even now in the midst of history of what God purposes for his creation—both spiritual and material—at the end of time. He is, as Paul puts it, "the first fruits of those who have died" (1 Cor. 15:20), and hence his body is an indication of what we can all hope for.

He ascended into heaven and is seated at the right hand of the Father

We recall that after having clarified the nature of the Son of God, the Creed states, simply enough, "He came down from heaven," implying that he came among us not by abandoning his transcendent state but by taking to himself a human manner of existence. Just after the statement of Resurrection faith, the Creed says, completing the cycle, "He ascended into heaven." This is the *exitus-reditus* (going out and coming back) rhythm of the Incarnation: he came down, and he went back up. The implication is that the humanity that he came down to embrace, he now brings up for deification. The Creed in this regard is simply imitating the hymn in the second chapter of the Letter of Paul to the Philippians: "[He] emptied himself, taking the form of a slave, being born in human likeness. . . . God also highly exalted him and gave him the name that is above every name" (Phil. 2:7, 9). The downward trajectory is the condition for the possibility of an upward trajectory; heaven came to meet earth, so that the earthly could become the heavenly; or according to the patristic formula cited above, "God became man that man might become God."

If we consult the very few texts in the New Testament that describe the Ascension itself—in the Gospels of Mark and Luke and in the Acts of the Apostles—we will most likely be disappointed by their lack of detail and their somewhat tensive relationship with one another. The so-called longer ending of Mark, which probably does not go back to the evangelist himself, says only, "So then the Lord Jesus, after he had spoken to them, was taken up into heaven and sat down at the right hand of God" (Mark 16:19). And St. Luke's Gospel tells us that Jesus led the disciples out to Bethany, blessed them, and then "withdrew from them and was carried up into heaven" (Luke 24:51); whereas the Acts of the Apostles, written by the same Luke, makes no mention of Bethany, but seems to situate Jesus and his disciples in Jerusalem, whence Jesus "was lifted up, and a cloud took him out of their sight" (Acts 1:9). For most of the history of Christianity, these were indeed taken as more or less literal accounts describing some "vertical movement" on the part of Jesus as he left this world. However, I do think it is fair to say that these brief statements are meant, above all, to convey the theological meaning of Jesus' definitive entry into the realm of God. It is according to that hermeneutic that I would like to address them.

The Ascension of Jesus signals the definitive end of Jesus' post-Resurrection appearances and the commencement of his operation from the properly heavenly sphere. It is crucial to remember, however, that this distantiation by no means amounts to an abandonment, but rather to an even more intense form of intimacy. To move into heaven, or the divine manner of existence, is not to move to another place, but to that arena of existence that stands outside of space. Paul Tillich refers to God's *Überräumlichkeit* (over-spacedness), and he insists that this transcendence to any particular space implies the capacity to be present to every space. This is what we mean when we say that God is "everywhere" or ubiquitous. Therefore, to say that Jesus has "ascended" to that sphere of existence is not to say that he has "gone away." It is to assert, if I can adopt a military metaphor, that he has journeyed to a higher point of vantage where he can see the entire field of battle and direct operations more efficaciously.

With this comparison in mind, we can understand why the Creed tightly juxtaposes the affirmation of the Ascension with the claim that Jesus "is seated at the right hand of the Father." To be at the right hand of the king and to be in the seated position is to have assumed the role of plenipotentiary, something like a prime minister or chief vizier. The point is that Jesus is ruling his Church, indeed ruling the entire world, with the full authority of the Father. From his heavenly throne, he sees all, directs all, and intends to draw all to himself. Though the explicit descriptions of the moment of Ascension are, as we saw, only few, there are numerous biblical references to the reign of Jesus. For example, when asked at his trial whether he is the Messiah, Jesus responded: "I am; and 'you will see the Son of Man seated at the right hand of the Power,' and 'coming with the clouds of heaven'" (Mark 14:62).

Though I have stressed that the Ascension of Jesus does not mean that the Lord has "gone away," I would like equally to stress that, in another sense, his Ascension does represent a kind of clearing of space for others to do his work here below. Precisely as embodied, Jesus does indeed exist in a kind of mutually exclusive relationship to other bodies. Thus, if he were still present on earth, he would crowd anyone else out of the position that he holds. Imagine what the political arena would be like if Lincoln, Churchill, Roosevelt, and Napoleon still strode the stage: there would be room for no one else. In this sense, the "disappearance" of the Lord from the stage of history enables others to imitate him in creative ways. It opens up the arena for the saints, who participate in his governance, each in a distinctive way.

So far, we have been discussing the Ascension of Jesus under the more or less "political" rubric of his reign, his active direction of his Church. But there is an equally important dimension of the ascended Christ's action—namely, the liturgical. We saw that the cross of Jesus must be understood as an act of priestly sacrifice. Representing the entire human race, Jesus offers his own body and blood to the Father; taking the role of the scapegoat, Jesus allows all of the sins of the world to be placed on his back in order that he might carry them away. When he passes judgment on the corrupt Jerusalem temple, just days before his death, he predicts that that great center of Jewish worship will be torn down but that he himself will rebuild it in three days. John's Gospel adds the interpretive gloss that he was speaking of the temple of his body. We must conclude that Jesus' crucified body is the new place where heaven and earth meet, and that the Lord acts as both sacrificing priest and sacrificed lamb.

The author of the Letter to the Hebrews, whose name and identity have been lost to us, was undoubtedly either a priest of the temple or someone intimately associated with the temple and its rituals, for he provides a richly liturgical interpretation of the essential activity undertaken by the ascended Christ. He signals his principal theme in chapter 4: "Since, then, we have a great high priest who has passed through the heavens, Jesus, the Son of God, let us hold fast to our confession" (Heb. 4:14). Having ascended to a transcendent realm (through the heavens), he functions in the manner of the high priest in the temple—which is to say, offering sacrifice for the reconciliation of God and his people.

But whereas the priesthood here below was inadequate to its task, now, in the resurrected and ascended Jesus, we have a morally and spiritually immaculate representative: "For it was fitting that we should have such a high priest, holy, blameless, undefiled, separated from sinners, and exalted above the heavens" (Heb. 7:26). Unlike the corrupt priests here below, this heavenly figure "has no need to offer sacrifices day after day, first for his own sins, and then for those of the people" (Heb. 7:27). He has, in point of fact, offered the perfect sacrifice on the cross once and for all—and this indeed historical act, since it belonged to a divine person, subsists in the eternal realm, beyond space and time and hence applicable to all space and all time.

This perfect high priest, having ascended to the heavenly temple, brings into the true Holy of Holies that of which the blood of thousands of sacrificed animals were but the symbol: "He entered once for all into the Holy Place, not with the blood of goats and calves, but with his own blood, thus obtaining eternal redemption. For if the blood of goats and bulls . . . sanctifies those who have been defiled . . . how much more will the blood of Christ . . . purify our conscience from dead works to worship the living God!" (Heb. 9:12–14). In a word, the Son's great act of obedience that took place on the cross now stands permanently in the presence of the Father as a sweet offering, effecting reconciliation. Jesus is the high priest on the Day of Atonement, but his sacrifice is perfect and has eternal validity, and the Holy of Holies that he has entered on our behalf is not an earthly simulacrum but the very dwelling place of God.

This same idea finds an imagistic counterpart in the book of Revelation. In chapter 4, the visionary author reports that "there in heaven a door stood open!" (Rev. 4:1). When he passes through, he sees a throne room that also seems to function as a sort of temple, for around the throne are gathered white-robed elders (the word here is *presbyteroi*, from which "priest" is derived), who engage in gestures and songs of worship: "Whenever the living creatures give glory and honor and thanks to the one who is seated on the throne ... the twenty-four elders fall before the one who is seated on the throne and worship the one who lives forever and ever" (Rev. 4:9–10). In the right hand of the one seated upon the throne, the visionary spies "a scroll written on the inside and on the back, sealed with seven seals" (Rev. 5:1). This might be construed as an account of all of history or the Scriptures themselves. A voice is heard asking, "Who is worthy to open the scroll and break its seals?" (Rev. 5:2). In other words, who can possibly provide the interpretive key to the mysteries of revelation and of history?

No one presents himself, and there is sadness in heaven, until there finally appears a peculiar figure, "a Lamb standing as if it had been slaughtered" (Rev. 5:6). This weakest of animals, this typical sacrificial victim, is evocative of Jesus, the one slain upon the cross for the sake of the world. But anomalously, he *stands*, indicating the enduring power of what he has accomplished. This lamb, standing though slain, takes the scroll from the hand of the King, and all of the heavenly court gathers around him, singing a hymn of praise: "You are worthy to take the scroll and to open its seals, for you were slaughtered and by your blood you ransomed for God saints from every tribe and language and people and nation; you have made them to be a kingdom and priests serving our God, and they will reign on earth" (Rev. 5:9–10). I have quoted this extraordinary passage at length, for it gathers, marvelously, so many of the themes that we have explored in relation to the Cross, Resurrection, and Ascension of Jesus.

And this brings us to the liturgical praise offered by the Church here below. From the beginning, Christian worship has had a transcendent orientation and a mystical meaning. That is to say, it is infinitely more than the gathering of like-minded people for the purpose of mutual support and shared praise; it is an act performed in conscious union with the saints and angels in heaven and under the headship of the ascended Christ. In the prayers of the Catholic liturgy, uttered just before the climactic Eucharistic Prayer, we find this language: "May our voices, we pray, join with [the angels] in one chorus of exultant praise." What follows is "Holy, Holy, Holy, Lord God of hosts. Heaven and earth are full of your glory. Hosanna in the highest." The triple holy is meant to evoke two great biblical texts, one from the Old Testament and one from the New Testament. The first is from the story in the sixth chapter of the book of the prophet Isaiah concerning the call of the prophet. While praying in the temple, he sees the glory of the Lord filling the place and he spies seraphs, the highest type of angels, singing to one another: "Holy, holy, holy is the LORD of hosts" (Isa. 6:3). The second reference is to the fourth chapter of Revelation, which describes the four living creatures around the throne echoing their counterparts in Isaiah: "Holy, holy, holy, the Lord God the Almighty, who was and is and is to come" (Rev. 4:8). Again, the prayers of worshipers here below are meant to "be one" with these prayers offered on high, the harmonious singing of heaven awakening the harmonious singing of the Church on earth.

And that we might keep the kingly and priestly

dimensions connected, we should never forget that this liturgical *communio* is meant to be the model and source of political, economic, and social *communio*, the prayer of the Church functioning, as Thomas Merton put it, as the "axle around which the whole country blindly turns." The right worship offered by the Christian Church—praise directed to the God of love and forgiveness—is the key to the creation of a just social order here below and ultimately an anticipation of the life that the blessed will live on high forever with God.

He will come again in glory

I spoke earlier of the *exitus-reditus* rhythm of the Incarnation, but I wonder whether an exhaustive account would not include a second *exitus*: the Son of God goes out, comes back, and then goes out again. He came once to earth (taking to himself a human nature), brought that nature glorified to heaven, and then will come again in order to glorify all of matter, all of space, and all of time. If the metaphor of coming and going and coming again is getting a little awkward, we could speak of the ascended Jesus, who is God and man, finally drawing all things to himself, so that earth and heaven meet in a marvelous *conubium* (marriage). Remember that at the heart of the prayer that Jesus taught his disciples is the petition that the will of God be done "on earth as it is in heaven" (Matt. 6:10). This implies not an escape from the earth to heaven but a coming together of the two dimensions in a kind of embrace.

This anticipation of a definitive salvation of creation itself is mentioned again and again in the New

Testament. In a series of supremely mysterious texts, St. Paul speaks, in his Letter to the Romans, of the longing of the universe for redemption: "We know that the whole creation has been groaning in labor pains until now" (Rom. 8:22). We find something similar in 2 Peter 3, where the author speaks of "the coming of the day of God," which will result in a passing away of the old order and the arrival of "new heavens and a new earth, where righteousness is at home" (2 Pet. 3:12–13). In the twenty-first chapter of the book of Revelation, we are told of the descent of the heavenly Jerusalem, the glorified city where perfect praise of God obtains in its every aspect, and accompanying this arrival is "a new heaven and a new earth" (Rev. 21:1).

That this cosmic renewal is centered around the very particular Jesus of Nazareth is made abundantly clear in Paul's Letter to the Colossians. In an astonishing hymn of praise in the opening chapter of that letter, Paul signals that Jesus is the one through whom the universe was made: "He is the image of the invisible God, the firstborn of all creation; for in him all things in heaven and on earth were created" (Col. 1:15–16); the one in whom it subsists: "He himself is before all things and in him all things hold together" (Col. 1:17); and the one by whom it will be brought to fulfillment: "For in him all the fullness of God was pleased to dwell, and through him God was pleased to reconcile to himself all things, whether on earth or in heaven" (Col. 1:19–20). The very same idea of universal reconciliation through Christ is unambiguously laid out in the opening chapter of Paul's missive to the church in Ephesus: "With all wisdom and insight he has made known to us the mystery of his will, according to his good pleasure that he set forth in Christ, as a plan for the fullness of time, to gather up all things in him, things in heaven and things on earth" (Eph. 1:8–10).

There are many other such texts that I could cite, but I trust the point has been made. The "coming again" of Jesus, for which the author of Revelation in practically the very last words of the Bible prays ("Come, Lord Jesus"), involves the elevation and glorification of the whole of God's creation. The Gnostic dream of escape from matter is just not at all what the Scriptures are interested in.

Now, what will this new heavens and new earth be like? No one knows with certitude. But can the resurrected Jesus give us at least a frame of reference? We saw earlier that the risen Lord is in clear continuity with the Jesus of the public ministry, but that he is also changed, transfigured. Thus, the new state of affairs will be, in a way, the same earth and the same heavens, but now lifted up to a condition of perfection. We might suggest that the new creation is to the old as a sphere is to a circle, or a pyramid to a triangle, or a box to a rectangle. In each of those cases, the more primitive shape is preserved, but it is enhanced, raised literally to a new dimension.

To judge the living and the dead

Having ensured that the cosmic aspect of this reconciliation is sufficiently emphasized, I should like to return to the particularly human arena, for the Creed says that the principal work of Christ, having come in glory, is "to judge the living and the dead." I wonder whether, within the horizon of our cultural assumptions, there is any article of the Creed more objectionable than this one. I say this because we, at least in the secularized West, are massively uncomfortable with the idea of judgment—at least we say we are. When practically every other moral value is relativized and subjectivized, we assume, as a sort of default position, that nonjudgmentalism is an objective and universal desideratum. We have become expert in the art of self-exculpation. The bad feelings and negative self-image that follow from judgment strike people today as so extraordinarily dangerous that practically no effort is spared to undermine it. That an outside agent would pronounce negatively on what a person says, does, or claims to be is construed as an inexcusable act of violence.

If all of this is true in regard to the judgment offered by one's fellow human beings, how much more problematic it becomes in regard to a judgment offered by God—which is to say, one that is definitive and that carries everlasting implications. By way of an initial response, I might point out the contradiction involved in most of the opposition to "judgmentalism." Those who are most vocal in protecting themselves and others from judgment are typically all too willing to judge, even harshly so, those who are not in agreement with them, a phenomenon all too familiar in the often brutally exclusive advocates of radical inclusion. We should simply face the fact that something like judgment is more or less unavoidable, no matter what position we take, for to set one's face is, necessarily, to set one's back. I will confess that it is with some amusement that I direct those who see Jesus as *the* model of inclusivity and nonjudgmentalism to the stark judgments that are found, fairly regularly, on the lips of that same Jesus.

And when we turn to the judgment of God, we should see that this divine discrimination should be, in fact, a source of vindication and comfort rather than dread. First, to say that God is the judge of truth and falsity, of right and wrong, of beauty and ugliness, is to acknowledge that God is the true, the good, and the beautiful in their properly unconditioned form. If this grounding criterion were removed, all values—moral, aesthetic, and rational—would become unmoored, and we would not be finally capable of determining and ordering what is objectively true or good. And as history makes painfully and abundantly clear, in that sort of epistemic and moral chaos, the will to power prevails and a strong man imposes order, following his own whim or fear. Within the Gospels, Pontius Pilate, indifferent to the truth, is the archetype in this regard.

We can make our analysis of the judgment of God more concrete by looking at the disconcerting fact that the world is a dark, violent, and deeply unjust place. Even the most casual survey of history and of the daily newspaper reveals that there have been and continue to be massive assaults on the dignity of human beings: murder, kidnapping, rape, genocide, slavery, human trafficking, pornography, imperialistic oppression, denial of fundamental rights, etc. These outrages quite rightly call forth the ameliorative efforts of decent people: police officers, journalists, judges and lawyers, social activists, military personnel, preachers, and politicians. Sometimes indeed, the interventions of such figures result in the righting of wrongs, the punishment of offenders, and the restoration of violated human dignity. But if we are honest, we must admit that far too frequently, injustice goes insufficiently answered within the lifetimes of the perpetrators or the offended parties. How many murders have remained permanently unsolved, how many broken lives permanently unrepaired, how many war-ravaged societies and psyches permanently compromised?

And so, by an altogether legitimate instinct, we say that all of these injustices "cry out to heaven for vengeance." Knowing full well that nothing here below can truly right these wrongs, and knowing furthermore that there is an objective standard for all of our moral judgments, we refer these sins to God; we bring them before God for final adjudication. Precisely because God is both unconditionally good and outside of the strictures of time, we can hope that all sins, even those lost in the mists of history, can be addressed, and all suffering, even of people long dead, can be soothed.

But this conviction is given further support and focus through the dying, rising, and ascending of the Son of God. As we saw, the Crucifixion of the sinless Lord was the greatest act of injustice possible, since it was tantamount to the killing of God. In it, we might say, all of the outrages and injustices of the world were contained, acknowledged, brought into the light. And then, in the Resurrection of the Son of God, all of that darkness was overcome, the *shalom* of the risen Jesus signaling the setting right of what was off-kilter. Finally, the Ascension, which entails the enthronement of that same Messiah, represents Jesus' lordship over space and time, his great ongoing work of reconciliation through his Mystical Body, the Church.

According to the Creed, this magnificent work of the ascended Christ involves, at the end of the day, the judging of the "living and the dead." The presumption is that when he comes—that is to say, when things are finally resolved—there will be some still living on the earth as well as an army of those who have died over the ages. All will be evaluated in terms of their relationship to Christ; all will be arranged, so to speak, properly under his headship.

And his kingdom will have no end

After affirming that Jesus will come as final judge, the Creed adds the tagline "And his kingdom will have no end." What is being asserted here is the participation of the new way of ordering things in the very eternity of God. When the new Jerusalem descends from heaven, or to shift the metaphor, when we go out to meet Christ in the air, the two realms of heaven and earth are joined in a kind of marriage. The entire drama of nature and history, which would have unfolded over eons of time, will come, finally, to an end, but not a dead end, not to a condition of stasis, but rather to "rest"—which is to say, a savoring of the supreme good. The Creed is insisting that history is neither pointless nor circular nor dully repetitive. Instead, it is moving, under the direction of the Holy Spirit, toward a fulfillment beyond what any philosopher or seer could imagine: the kingdom without end.

4

The Holy Spirit

I believe in the Holy Spirit, the Lord, the giver of life

AFTER A RELATIVELY BRIEF DECLARATION of belief in the Father, and a far longer, more elaborated declaration of belief in the Son, the Creed articulates the Christian belief in the third person of the Trinity, the Holy Spirit. Like the *Commedia* of Dante, the *Summa theologiae* of Aquinas, and Chartres Cathedral, the Nicene Creed is essentially Trinitarian in structure and purpose.

So who or what is the *Pneuma to Hagion*, the *Spiritus Sanctus*, the Holy Breath in which we are professing our faith? I suppose the first clarification we should make is that the Holy Spirit is definitely a "who" rather than a "what," despite the rather impersonal descriptor. The reason is that the Creed immediately refers to the Spirit as "Lord." This personalizes him, of course, and also links the Holy Spirit to the Son of God, whom the Creed calls the "Lord Jesus Christ"; and, in one deft move, it unambiguously affirms the deity of the Spirit, for "Lord" is a term used, again and again, of the God of Israel.

The Creed gives us another crucially important indicator when it speaks of the Spirit as *zōopoion* (giver of life). As we saw when considering the Incarnation, the *ruach Yahweh*, the breath of God, is what brooded over the surface of the stormy waters at the moment of creation. All the vitality that came forth from the Creator issued from this ultimate source of life. In the thirty-seventh chapter of the book of the prophet Ezekiel, we find the beautiful and mysterious passage concerning the vivification of the dry bones. The prophet looks out on a field filled with the desiccated remains of soldiers, and he is told by God to speak to them. When Ezekiel speaks, the *ruach* of God stirs the bones and then covers them in sinew, muscle, and skin, and finally breathes life into them, causing them to stand up as a revivified army. So the Holy Spirit operates in and for the holy people Israel. The prophet Isaiah anticipates the coming Messiah, commenting, "The spirit of the LORD shall rest on him, the spirit of wisdom and understanding, the spirit of counsel and might, the spirit of knowledge and the fear of the LORD" (Isa. 11:2). And in Psalm 104, after exulting in the myriad ways that God brings forth life and fecundity, the Psalmist comments, "When you send forth your spirit, they are created; and you renew the face of the ground" (Ps. 104:30). There are many more examples I could cite from the Old Testament—in fact, the word *ruach* is used 378 separate times in the Hebrew Scriptures—but this should suffice to show that the Spirit is a divine source of life in multiple senses of the term: physical, moral, intellectual, and corporate.

When we turn to the New Testament, we find a plethora of references to the spirit and the Holy Spirit—indeed, the word *pneuma* is found there 385 times—and these retain their Old Testament sense of life-source, but now they are intensely concentrated around Jesus and the very particular kind of life that comes from and through him. We can see the Spirit's influence throughout the career of Jesus. Thus, in Luke's infancy narrative, we hear the angel tell the puzzled Mary that "the Holy Spirit will come upon you, and the power of the Most High will overshadow you" (Luke 1:35). At the Lord's baptism, the Spirit appears in the form of a dove to John the Baptist, who exclaims, "I myself did not know him, but the one who sent me to baptize with water said to me, 'He on whom you see the Spirit descend and remain is the one who baptizes with the Holy Spirit'" (John 1:33). And after his Resurrection, Jesus appeared to his disciples, breathed on them, evoking thereby the great Old Testament symbol of the *ruach Yahweh*, and said, "Receive the Holy Spirit. If you forgive the sins of any, they are forgiven them; if you retain the sins of any, they are retained" (John 20:22–23).

The explosive arrival of the Holy Spirit in the midst of the gathered disciples, which calls to mind so many of the symbols associated with the Spirit in the Old Testament, is described by St. Luke in the Acts of the Apostles. "When the day of Pentecost had come, they were all together in one place. And suddenly from heaven there came a sound like the rush of a violent wind, and it filled the entire house where they were sitting. . . . All of them were filled with the Holy Spirit and began to speak in other languages, as the Spirit gave them ability" (Acts 2:1–2, 4). Those in the upper room were like the dead bones described by Ezekiel, and the Spirit of Jesus stirred them to life, indeed made them a powerful army, ready to go forth.

Then, in the aftermath of Pentecost, the Spirit is unleashed upon the world. He guides, bears witness, prays, teaches, speaks, converts, lifts up, inspires, and directs. St. Paul claims that all of the power and persuasiveness of his preaching comes not from his own wise words or clever rhetoric but from the Holy Spirit: "My speech and my proclamation were not with plausible words of wisdom, but with a demonstration of the Spirit and of power" (1 Cor. 2:4). In a curious passage from the Acts of the Apostles, the Holy Spirit seems involved very personally in the deliberations of the Council of Jerusalem. The protagonists conclude: "For it has seemed good to the Holy Spirit and to us to impose on you no further burden than these essentials . . ." (Acts 15:28). We might go so far as to say that the Holy Spirit is the principal actor in the life of the early Church, always keeping in mind the principle of noncompetitiveness, so that his activity in no way obviates or interrupts the real activity of the disciples of Jesus.

Therefore, we might sum up as follows: the Holy Spirit is the creative, life-giving power of the God of Israel that was involved in a completely unique way with Jesus from the very beginning of his earthly life, which filled him with fire and wisdom, which animated his ministry, and which he was able to give, after his Resurrection, generously to his Church. But what is the nature of this life? What precisely is it that Jesus had in such a distinctively unique manner and that he now offers as a gift to his followers?

Who proceeds from the Father and the Son, who with the Father and the Son is adored and glorified

To answer these questions, we need to turn to the next line of the Creed and explore it with the help of the theological tradition: "who proceeds from the Father and the Son." The shared love between Father and Son—the "sigh" of love between them, as Fulton Sheen memorably put it—is the *Spiritus Sanctus*, the Holy Breath. Recall that to love is to will the good of the other as other. If there is even a modicum of self-interest on the part of the one who wills, true love disappears and becomes at least indirect egotism. In point of fact, some postmodern theorists have argued that a real gift, for this very reason, is impossible, for to be authentic it must involve absolutely no expectation of reciprocity. Yet, it appears that any gift has to awaken in the recipient some sense of obligation, even as slight as the obligation of gratitude. But these dynamics do not apply to God, since he is utterly perfect and hence needs nothing. Since the Father and the Son share the one divine essence, neither can possibly "benefit" from the other, and therefore neither can experience self-interest, either direct or indirect. Thus, their shared willing is the purest love possible, the very essence of love.

Once again, lest there be any ambiguity on this score, given the divine simplicity, whatever is attributed to God is identical to the divine essence. Hence, the love proceeding from the Father and the Son is fully divine. He therefore should not be construed along the lines of an act of the will that is but an expression of an underlying consciousness. It is not one thing that God happens to do, but rather God himself. And thus the Creed is correct to specify that the Holy Spirit "with the Father and the Son is adored and glorified." Unlike mere reverence or honor, adoration is uniquely directed to God.

What are we sensing in the rapport between Jesus and his Father but precisely this divine love? In the conversation between the Sender and the One Sent—a conversation that is the Holy Spirit—we find an icon of the love that obtains in God from all eternity. "God so loved the world that he gave his only Son, so that everyone who believes in him may not perish but may have eternal life" (John 3:16). That famous passage from John's Gospel presents the Trinitarian persons admirably, God (the Father) sending the Son precisely out of the love that proceeds from and connects them—namely, the Holy Spirit. And just to make the icon complete, we see that the purpose of this mission is none other than the gathering of the human race into the Trinitarian life, into the love between the Father and the Son. That is the life that Jesus shares. That is what he bequeaths to his Church and through his Church to the world: the capacity to love in the utterly disinterested way that the Trinity loves.

Now that these essential elements are in place, we can articulate an at least relatively adequate conceptual account of the Trinity. As we learned from the first line of the Nicene Creed, God is one. At no point does Christian teaching involve a compromising of the fierce monotheism of Israel. The divine essence is one. But because God is all-knowing, he is unconditionally present to himself. He utters an interior Word, completely reflective of his own reality, and therefore, it is appropriate for us to speak of the Father (the Speaker) and the Son (the Word spoken), of the unoriginate and the begotten, both of whom share the one divine essence. And because God's knowledge is unconditioned, he knows himself as good and hence loves what he has understood, and because the Son shares perfectly in the Father's way of being, the Son looks back at the Father and loves what he knows. Therefore, along with the unoriginated and the begotten, we must posit the "spirated"—which is to say, the one breathed back and forth (*spirare* in Latin) between the Father and the Son.

Thus, we have one God and two separate processions, that of the Son from the Father and that of the Holy Spirit from the Father and the Son. And we have identified three within the unity of God—namely, the unbegotten principle of divinity, the begotten internal Word, and the spirated love between them. For want of a better term, we refer to these three realities as "persons." In making what might appear a tossed-off remark, I am imitating St. Augustine who, when musing why we call the Father, Son, and Holy Spirit persons, said that it was so we have something to say when people ask us what they are. In a similar vein, St. Anselm characterized them as *tres nescio quid* (three I don't know whats)! Both Augustine and Anselm realized the serious danger that the word "person" gives the impression of a separately existing and subsistent being. If there are three persons in the room, there are three individuals in the room—and this is precisely what we do not want to communicate in regard to the Trinitarian threesome.

Some nine centuries after Augustine and two centuries after Anselm, Thomas Aquinas engaged in a pretty impressive act of metaphysical poetry and referred to the Trinitarian persons as "subsistent relations." In terms of classical ontology, he was speaking nonsense, for subsistence belongs to substances (those things that exist through themselves) and relations are categorized as accidents (modifications of substances). Therefore, the two terms are mutually exclusive. The one thing that relations do not do is subsist; they inhere in something else. However, the demands of Trinitarian metaphysics compelled Aquinas to break the categories, something in the manner of a physicist saying that light is both wave and particle. The Father, Son, and Holy Spirit are certainly not modifications of the substance "God," for that would compromise the divine simplicity; and yet they are not separate beings, for that would result in tri-theism, compromising the divine unity. They are, we are forced to say, "pure" relations subsisting *as* relations. Thus, the Father is Father only in and *as* a relation to the Son; the Son is Son only in and *as* a relation to the Father; and the Spirit is Spirit only in and *as* a relation to the Father and the Son.

Perhaps at this juncture, it would be advisable to address the famous (infamous?) *filioque* controversy. I will admit I am reluctant to do so, because I am convinced that there is ultimately nothing to it and that it gives dogmatic theology a bad reputation for logic-chopping and hairsplitting. However, it has figured prominently in the history of the roiled relationship between the Eastern and Western branches of Christianity and continues to be a stumbling block to unification. Exploring the details and intricacies of the debate would be tiresome and would take us way too far afield; therefore, allow me to lay out the matter somewhat economically. In the original version of the great Creed under consideration—that is to say, the Nicene-Constantinopolitan statement of 381—we read that the Holy Spirit "*ek tou Patros ekporeuomenon*" (came forth from the Father). This formulation reflects the statement of Jesus in the fifteenth chapter of John's Gospel to the effect that "when the Advocate comes, whom I will send to you from the Father, the Spirit of truth who *comes from the Father* . . ." (John 15:26).

However, others, especially in the Western part of the Church, began to think that many scriptural passages seemed to imply that the Spirit was sent from both the Father and the Son. Time and again, St. Paul refers to the Holy Spirit as the Spirit of Jesus Christ, and even in the citation above, the Lord indicates that he will send the Spirit along with the Father. And according to the principle that dictates that the "economic" Trinity (the missions of the persons in the history of salvation) reflects truths within the "immanent" Trinity (the relations of the persons from all eternity), it seems that the Spirit comes forth from the Father and the Son acting in tandem. And so at the local Third Council of Toledo in 589, the Latin phrase *filioque* (and from the Son) was added to the Nicene-Constantinopolitan formula. When Charlemagne came to power around the year 800, this version of the Creed with the *filioque* became standardized at liturgies throughout much of Western Christianity.

Understandably, many in the East were outraged that a statement of the faith as venerable and ecumenical as the Nicene-Constantinopolitan Creed had been tinkered with by a local synod. More to it, theologians from the Eastern tradition were deeply concerned that making the Son a common source, with the Father, of the Spirit fatally compromised the primacy of the Father within the Trinitarian life. Another concern was that giving the Son the same generating power as the Father vis-à-vis the Holy Spirit would seem to put the Spirit in a position subordinate to the Father and the Son. If one were to insist on a role for the Son in the coming forth of the Spirit, the Eastern theologians were willing to speak of the Spirit coming from the Father *through* the Son.

Rising to the challenge, theologians in the West countered that the *filioque* honored the complexity of the biblical witness and assured the tight link between the Spirit and the Son. Moreover, the great psychological analogy provided by Augustine, the most influential of the Western Fathers, was especially congruent with the *filioque*, since, on his reading, the Spirit is indeed breathed out by both the Father and Son operating in tandem. The Eastern concerns about denigrating the primacy of the Father, Thomas Aquinas argued, are unfounded, in the measure that whatever the Son has, including his capacity to co-spirate the Spirit, came forth in procession from the Father. Finally, a careful reading of such Eastern masters as John Damascene and Maximus the Confessor appears to indicate that everything the West means by *filioque* is implied in the "through the Son" favored by the East.

My personal recommendation is that this controversy, which is at least as much political as theological, should be laid to rest permanently. Both the Orthodox and Catholic traditions believe in the unity of God, the coequality of the Trinitarian persons, and the unoriginated primacy of the Father. In regard to the *filioque*, the

West should say to the East, "What you mean by taking it out, we mean by putting it in," and the East should say to the West, "What you mean by putting it in, we mean by taking it out." Then both sides should declare victory and go home.

Still, under the rubric of determining what precisely this life is that Jesus communicates to his Church, I should like to return to the Bible, in fact to one of the most remarkable passages in the New Testament: the so-called Farewell Discourse offered by Jesus the night of the Last Supper, which culminates in his "high priestly" oration. Covering practically the whole of chapters 14–17 of John's Gospel, this speech constitutes, by far, the longest and most theologically dense utterance of Jesus anywhere in the Gospels—and its focus is the dynamics within the inner life of the Trinity. After clarifying that he himself is the way that conduces to the Father and that the one who sees him indeed sees the Father, Jesus commences to speak of the Holy Spirit: "And I will ask the Father, and he will give you another Advocate, to be with you forever. This is the Spirit of truth, whom the world cannot receive, because it neither sees him nor knows him" (John 14:16–17). The term for "Advocate" that the Lord uses here in the Greek is *Parakletos*, which has the literal sense of "calling to one's side," and hence means something like helper or advocate, someone who will speak on behalf of another in the manner of a lawyer.

What this advocacy involves is laid out just a few verses later when Jesus declares, "I have said these things to you while I am still with you. But the Advocate [*Parakletos*], the Holy Spirit, whom the Father will send in my name, will teach you everything, and remind you of all that I have said to you" (John 14:25–26). And lest there be any misunderstanding, he specifies in chapter 16: "I still have many things to say to you, but you cannot bear them now. When the Spirit of truth comes, he will guide you into all the truth" (John 16:12–13). We see in these fascinating passages, first, that the Holy Spirit works in tight connection with Jesus, and second, that the truth implicit in the teaching of Jesus requires the ministrations of the Spirit to come to fully developed expression. The Advocate will never work at cross-purposes to Jesus and what is revealed in him, but he does indeed represent an element of freedom and novelty. The Spirit, to use Karl Barth's language, is the Interpreter of the Word, monitoring its development throughout the course of the Church's life.

Who has spoken through the prophets

Now we can understand more clearly what the Creed means when it says, so simply and profoundly, that the Holy Spirit has "spoken through the prophets." Like Judaism and Islam, Christianity is a prophetic religion— which is to say, a religion that depends not so much on the rational musings of its adepts, but upon the word uttered by certain distinctive figures who made bold to speak not just *about* God but in the very *name* of God and under his authority. The prophets of the Old Testament were seized by a power beyond themselves and were commanded to speak, very often against their wills. Jeremiah famously protested, "Ah, Lord GOD! Truly I do not know how to speak, for I am only a boy" (Jer. 1:6), and Isaiah, upon being called, complained, "Woe is me! I am lost, for I am a man of unclean lips, and I live among a people of unclean lips" (Isa. 6:5). This reluctance indicates that the prophet is decidedly not like a philosopher or social activist, operating on his own initiative and according to his own ideas of the good.

The prophet does not necessarily foretell the future, though this can be a function of his fundamental mission. His basic task is, as Yves Congar puts it, to speak God's judgment on things—which is to say, to evaluate the affairs of the world from the perspective of God and God's purposes. What the world tends to treat as ends—power, privilege, wealth, fame, etc.—the prophet sees as, at best, means to an end and, at worst, obstacles to achieving the only end worth achieving, which is doing the will of God. This transvaluation of values is what gives so many of the prophets—think especially of Amos, Hosea, and Zechariah in this context—their cutting, critical edge. It also helps to explain why so many of them ended up persecuted, rejected, or put to death. Abraham Joshua Heschel, one of the twentieth century's great scholars of biblical prophecy, said that the prophet is someone who feels the feelings of God and then speaks out of that experience. In light of this description, one thinks of the way in which these spokespeople for the Lord channeled God's anger, his passion to set things right, his delight, his encouragement, etc. The prophets are frequently ahead of their time, for they see where God is tending and hence they push people and institutions beyond their comfortable status quo.

This is what leads to a tension we find frequently in both the Bible and the history of the Church between prophecy and ritualism or institutionalism. André

Rousseaux, in a work on Charles Péguy, expressed the stress this way: "The prophet always sees the opposite of everybody else: he reverses the apparent order of things that is actually false, and rediscovers the real order." Very much in the same spirit, Chesterton commented that the fool for Christ stands on his head and hence sees everything as upside down. But since this inversion of vision takes place in a world already upside down due to the effects of sin, Christ's fool actually sees things aright.

Now, it is important to note that the tension ought not to turn into a contradiction, for the prophetic perspective, in time and usually after a great deal of struggle and opposition, does become settled teaching. The Gospel of John presents this relationship symbolically in the race of John and Peter to the tomb of Christ on Easter Sunday morning. The prophetic visionary got to the tomb first, but then waited for the official leader to catch up and to verify what the prophet had seen.

Prophecy continues, quite obviously, in the New Testament and in the early Church. Jesus never objected to being called "prophet," and many of his words and actions were congruent with his Old Testament prophetic forebears. The Apostles, filled with the Spirit at Pentecost, certainly preached and wrote in the manner of the prophets, and their teaching came, early on, to be established as authoritative in the life of the Church. And thus it is not surprising that the doctrine articulated by their successors the bishops became normative for the Christian community.

To be sure, up and down the ages, the settled doctrine was sometimes challenged by prophetic figures, some of whom were deemed too extreme, but others of whom were accepted as fomenters of legitimate development and whose critiques, accordingly, were integrated at length into the doctrinal tradition. John Henry Newman, in fact, holds that the prophetic office, broadly interpreted, includes theologians, teachers, writers, and mystics, who sift through the received teaching of the Church and place it in dialogue with the ever-changing cultural situation. It is precisely this open-ended, sometimes chaotic conversation that prompts the development of doctrine—and to be fair, the corruption of it as well. What is required is the refereeing office of the bishops and the pope, which operates, under the Holy Spirit, so as to determine the difference.

It is often commented that the Church is not a democracy, and this is meant in several senses. Under this rubric of prophecy, it means that the teaching of the Church does not emerge as a consensus of the people, as the distillate of the common religious experience. It comes rather from certain very definite and rare individuals who received the grace to speak from the perspective of God. At the risk of proposing a metaphor that will be taken in a purely political sense, the doctrine of Christianity does not come "from below," but rather "from above," from the Holy Spirit who deigned (and deigns) to speak "through the prophets."

5

The Church

I believe in

WHAT ONE SHOULD NOTICE FIRST in regard to this article of the Creed is the peculiarity of using the word "believe" when the object of that belief is an institution, the Church. It seems altogether appropriate that we should express our faith in the Father, the Son, and the Holy Spirit, since these are all divine persons. But is it not at least questionable, at worst idolatrous, to be professing *belief* in the Church? It would be, of course, if the Church were nothing but a human institution, nothing other than an aggregation of like-minded people, nothing more than an assembly born of the common will of those who belong to it.

The use of the term "believe" in this context signals perhaps the most fundamental truth regarding the Church—namely, that it is a sacrament of Christ and hence, in a very real fashion, that it participates in Christ's divinity. We saw that the Incarnation involves the eternal Son of God taking to himself a human nature to use as his iconic manifestation, or in the more technical language of Thomas Aquinas, as his *instrumentum*. The glorified and ascended body of Jesus of Nazareth exists now in the realm of God, but the Son of God resolved to take to himself another Body, this one spreading across space and time, made up of all of those grafted onto Christ through Baptism. This Body—and it is St. Paul who first suggested that seminal image to us—would now be the *instrumentum* through which Christ would continue his work in the world. Hence, the Church in which we quite rightly *believe* should not be compared to an organization, though it has, as we shall see, institutional features, but rather to an organism. Summing up much theological speculation from the previous century and a half, the Second Vatican Council, in its document on the Church, entitled *Lumen Gentium*, states, "By communicating His Spirit, Christ made His brothers, called together from all nations, mystically the components of His own Body."

There are, of course, many biblical warrants besides the epistles of Paul for this association. When the risen Jesus speaks to Saul on the road to Damascus, he says, "Saul, Saul, why do you persecute *me*?" (Acts 9:4). Saul, of course, was en route to arrest and round up followers of Jesus, and yet the Lord refers to this act as an offense against *himself*. In Matthew 25, we find the famous parable of the sheep and the goats. When Christ the judge determines, at the end of time, who will come with him and who will be excluded, he makes the discrimination on the basis of how each person treated the sick, the hungry, the imprisoned, and the naked. He says to the blessed, "Truly I tell you, just as you did it to one of the least of these who are members of my family, you did it *to me*" (Matt. 25:40). And to the cursed, "Truly I tell you, just as you did not do it to one of the least of these, you did not do it *to me*" (Matt. 25:45).

Perhaps the clearest indication of the intimate rapport that obtains between Jesus and his Body the Church is found toward the end of the Farewell Discourse, parts of which we analyzed in the last chapter, when Jesus offers his high priestly prayer. Addressing his Father directly, Jesus the Son prays for his Apostles and for those who would follow them down through the centuries: "I ask not only on behalf of these, but also on behalf of those who will believe in me through their word, that they may all be one. As you, Father, are in me and I am in you, may they also be in us, so that the world may believe that you have sent me" (John 17:20–21). What is most extraordinary in this passage is the clear implication that, precisely as the Mystical Body of Jesus, the Church is drawn into the inner life of the Trinity, sharing in the oneness enjoyed by the three persons of God. We see now why any account of the Church that construes it as a mere human collectivity, as the "Jesus Christ Society," is pitifully inadequate. It would be far more accurate to see it as the prolongation of the Incarnation across space and time.

John Henry Newman makes this point through a lovely reflection on the story of Jesus telling Mary Magdalene on Easter morning not to cling to him. Christ's words, Newman says, should not be seen as an off-putting remonstration, but as an invitation to come into an even more vibrant contact with his Mystical Body: "When I am thus changed, when I am thus present to you, more really present than now, though invisibly, then you may touch Me—may touch Me, more really though invisibly, by faith, in reverence, through such outward approaches as I shall assign."

If Christ Jesus is Head of this Mystical Body, then all those who are members of it through Baptism are cells, tissues, and organs, interdependently related to one another through him. This is why the suffering of any member of that Body is the suffering of every other, and why the triumph of any member is the triumph of every other. What Charles Williams called co-inherence—existing one in the other, each for the other—applies *par excellence* to the life of the Church. It is why such practices as praying for one another or offering one's suffering on behalf of another are metaphysically grounded and not empty pious gestures. Tertullian's famous observation that what attracted so many pagans in the early centuries of the Church's life was the concrete love that believers displayed—"How [these Christians] love one another!"—was made possible by this organic understanding of the Mystical Body.

It is sometimes suggested that Catholics place an obstacle between believers and Christ Jesus since they posit the institution of the Church as mediator. Would it not be better, more spiritually enlivening, to cultivate a direct relationship with the Lord and to construe the Church as indeed a society freely entered into by one's fellow believers, yet altogether subordinate to the personal friendship with Jesus? Again, for Catholics, such an objection is absurd, precisely because we do not understand the Church as "mediating" the relationship with Jesus any more than the body of the historical Christ "mediated" his relationships with Peter, James, John, or Mary Magdalene. In fact, St. Joan of Arc went so far as to say this in response to interrogators at her trial inquiring about her views on the relationship between Christ and the Church: "About Jesus Christ and the Church, I simply know they're just one thing, and we shouldn't complicate the matter."

If the Church is a Body and Christ is the Head, then

the Holy Spirit is the soul that animates the Body. We recall the scene described in John's Gospel when the risen Jesus, the night of Easter, breathed on his disciples, saying, "Receive the Holy Spirit" (John 20:22). This is precisely analogous to the Genesis account of Yahweh breathing his *ruach*, his life-giving Spirit, into the lifeless clay of Adam's body. The sending of the Spirit, fully expressed on Pentecost, is what made the Mystical Body into a living organism, and it is the continued presence of the Spirit that vivifies and makes fruitful the life of the Church to the present day. When it teaches, when it governs, when it sanctifies, when it manifests charisms of prophecy and healing, when it leads people to eternal life, the Church is making manifest its inner vitality.

We can discover a good deal about the Church's nature and mission by doing a simple etymological analysis of the relevant Greek word used in the Nicene Creed. What we believe in is the *ekklesia*, a word that in the ordinary parlance of the time designated simply a gathering or a society. It is derived from two terms: *ek* (from) and *kalein* (to call). Hence, an *ekklesia* is a group that has been called out from something into something else, that has been set apart.

So in regard to the *ekklesia* under consideration, we have to ask three questions: Who does the calling? What are its members being called out of? And what are they being called into? From the foregoing, it should be clear that the caller is Christ himself. Just as he summoned the original Twelve, and gathered in Zacchaeus, Bartimaeus, Nicodemus, Mary Magdalene, and the man born blind, so he continues, up and down the centuries, to call people to himself. We remember Jesus' clear insistence: "You did not choose me but I chose you" (John 15:16). Even those who enter the Church as adults, and who therefore do so as an act of their own will, are choosing to respond to a more primordial invitation.

What are members of the *ekklesia* called from? They are called, if I may use the biblical term, from "the world." This has nothing to do, of course, with a Platonic or Gnostic flight from matter and history. In the scriptural sense that I am using it, *kosmos* (world) designates the set of assumptions and manner of life animated by sin. Hence, "If my kingdom were from this *kosmos*, my followers would be fighting to keep me from being handed over" (John 18:36); and, "This is the Spirit of truth, whom the *kosmos* cannot receive, because it neither sees him nor knows him" (John 14:17). Thus, members of the Church are called out of a fallen way of thinking, feeling, perceiving, and behaving. They are invited to leave a world characterized by self-love and by the worship of false claimants to absolute status, out of the realm of kingdoms that belong to the scatterer (*diabolos*) and the accuser (*Satanas*).

One of the Old Testament figures that our tradition has taken as especially emblematic of the Church is Noah. At a time when the *tohu wabohu* of sin threatened the entire world, God noticed the righteous man, Noah. He commanded this one remaining servant of his to construct a great ship on which Noah's family and representatives of the entire animal kingdom would be invited to weather the storm. The Church Fathers saw Noah's ark as a particularly rich symbol of the *ekklesia*. In the midst of a crisis prompted by sin, God called out a remnant of his good creation and carefully preserved them from destruction. And so he continues to summon a relatively small community and to shape it as a people after his mind and heart. The time aboard that boat—cramped, anxious, unpleasant—evokes the permanent condition of the Church here below, which has not yet completed its voyage through space and time. Picking up on this patristic theme, the builders of the Gothic cathedrals endeavored to design their structures in such a way as to suggest the ark of Noah, making them look and feel like places of shelter in the storm.

So Christ calls his holy people out of the *tohu wabohu* of sin, but he never calls them for their own sake, and the Noah narrative helps us to see this with particular clarity. Once the waters receded, and the ark came to rest, Noah let out the life, releasing all of the animals, and his own family, to reinhabit the earth and to "be fruitful and multiply." Thus, the election of Noah was not for his own sake, but for the sake of the world. He was singled out not for his own aggrandizement, but rather for mission on behalf of others. The same rhythm can be seen, of course, in the stories of Abraham and Moses—and indeed in the stories of every person ever addressed by God in the Bible. No one—not Samuel, not Joshua, not David, not Jeremiah, not Isaiah, not Daniel—is given an experience of the Lord without being, as a consequence, sent. And thus the Church, the spiritual descendant of all of these figures, the institutional embodiment of Noah's ark, is indeed called *from* the world *for* the world.

And with that clarification, we have essentially answered the third question. The Church is called ultimately into the fullness of life and love that will obtain in heaven, but for the historical moment, it is called into permanent mission. Perhaps the central insight of Pope St. Paul VI's apostolic exhortation *Evangelii Nuntiandi* is that the Church does not *have* a mission alongside of myriad other projects; rather, it *is* a mission, by its very nature. In the language of the Second Vatican Council, it is meant to be the bearer of the *lumen* (the light of Christ Jesus himself) to the *gentes* (the nations). Pope Francis has been particularly eloquent on this score, insisting that a Church that fusses primarily with its own inner life has fallen into corruption. Expanding upon the biblical image of the oil that runs down the beard of Aaron and onto the collar of his robe, Francis says that the oil, which is a symbol of the Holy Spirit, ought to extend to the very fringes of the robe and thereby come into contact with the wider world. When the anointing does not flow out, it becomes rancid, a symbol of ecclesial introversion.

One

Having examined the *ekklesia*, at least in general outline, let us turn to the four qualities of the Church explicitly mentioned in the Nicene Creed: one, holy, catholic, and apostolic. The Church is one because God is one and God is using the Church to draw the whole human family into the divine life. If there were many absolutes, then we could imagine a variety of equally valid spiritual paths. If there were a plethora of gods, then it would make sense to have a plethora of churches. But that kind of pluralism in regard to the highest truth and goodness is inimical to the Scriptures and to the understanding of God as the unconditioned reality. In the Bible, God is presented consistently as a gathering force, drawing a people Israel to himself so that, through them, he might eventually gather in all the nations. "In days to come the mountain of the LORD's house shall be established as the highest of the mountains, and shall be raised above the hills; all the nations shall stream to it" (Isa. 2:2). Drawing at least implicitly on this Isaian theme, Jesus says in John's Gospel, "And I, when I am lifted up from the earth, will draw all people to myself" (John 12:32).

Nowhere is the all-embracing quality of the Church of Jesus given richer expression than in the first chapter of Paul's Letter to the Ephesians: "God put this power to work in Christ when he raised him from the dead and seated him at his right hand in the heavenly places, far above all rule and authority and power and dominion, and above every name that is named. . . . And he has put all things under his feet and has made him the head over all things for the church, which is his body, the fullness of him who fills all in all" (Eph. 1:20–23). This magnificent quotation, which brings together so many themes that we have explored in this book, indicates that the oneness of the Church is a function of the Church's identity as Christ's Body. Since Jesus is the force through which the Father is gathering all of humanity to himself, and since the Church is Christ's very Body, then the Church participates in the "all in all" character of its Lord.

In our postmodern period, this sort of claim, I realize, meets with immediate and intense resistance, for the valorization of pluralism in all things is taken for granted and, concomitantly, the shadow side of unity—namely, imperialistic oppression—is constantly brought to the fore. Any intellectual system, political arrangement, or especially religion that claims absolute or exclusive status is suspected, *ipso facto*, of aggression. The "masters of suspicion"—that is to say, Marx, Nietzsche, and Freud—have taught everyone, from the avatars of the high culture to high school students, to be wary of any ideology that would expect "all things to be drawn to itself."

Permit me to make two basic remarks in response to this concern. First, we must remember that the one who, on the Christian reading, is drawing all people to himself is none other than the crucified Jesus of Nazareth, the victim of an oppressive political and cultural system, who met his persecutors with nonviolence and forgiving love. I believe that a very persuasive argument could be made that the postmodern preoccupation with institutions of oppression is derived, ultimately, from the influence of Christian ethical principles flowing from the extraordinary witness of Jesus himself. Therefore, though it is a rather high paradox, the insistence that all things should be brought under the feet of Christ Jesus is not a power play—just the contrary. It is the privileging of the victim, the implicit criticism of all systems of violence and oppression. That the Church at times throughout its long history has acted at cross purposes to its own nature and imitated the worst of imperialistic regimes goes without saying, but these aberrations should not justify a demonization of the Church as inevitably imperious and domineering.

Secondly, the unity that the Church, at its best, is fostering is not monolithic but assimilating. Even the most cursory glance at the Church's life reveals that it is marked by extraordinary variety. There are multiple schools of spirituality and theology; innumerable orders, congregations, and societies; diverse styles of expression;

as many ways of being a saint as there are saints. The Church has been able to take into itself countless forms of life and adapt them to its essential structure. Moreover, as it has made its way through the centuries and across the globe, the Church has assimilated to itself a manifold of philosophies, religious practices, and cultural forms, even as it has resisted others. Thus, Origen, Gregory of Nyssa, Augustine, Anselm, and Bonaventure assimilated the work of Plato; missionaries to Ireland adapted certain expressions of Irish paganism to Christianity, even as missionaries to Germanic lands did the same with the religious forms that they discovered among the people they evangelized; etc.

Once again, I am not for a moment claiming that, in its long history, the Church always got this right, but I am indeed insisting that its characteristic instinct has not been to demolish what is other, but rather to draw it, as much as it reasonably can, into its own unity. The master image here is an animal making its way through its environment. If the animal is utterly resistant to what surrounds it, it will, in short order, die; by the same token, if it is utterly acquiescent to what surrounds it, it will also, just as rapidly, perish. The survival of the creature is a function of its ability to resist what it must and take in what it should in order to preserve its integrity and identity. The Church's unity is a function of just that sort of assimilating suppleness.

Holy

The second mark of the Church to which the Nicene Creed draws our attention is holiness. In the Old Testament, *kadosh* (holy) has the sense of "set apart." Thus, the angels that appear in Isaiah's great temple vision sing *kadosh, kadosh, kadosh*, signaling the strangeness and transcendence of the God of Israel. The holiness of the Church follows, then, from its identity as the vehicle by which Israel's God is gathering people into his distinctive form of life. To put this in more explicitly Christological terms, it is a concomitant of the nature of the Church as the Mystical Body of Jesus, set apart from any other corporate identity. This sense of the holy as the "separate" fits well with the notion that the *ekklesia* has been called out of false forms of community into something altogether new and different.

We saw that the Mystical Body has a soul—namely, the Holy Spirit—and just as we say that it is the soul that makes a person holy, so the Holy Spirit, which dwells perpetually in the Church, is what makes it holy. The Spirit's presence is manifested in the sacraments of the Church, in its official preaching, in its magisterial pronouncements and conciliar statements, in the charisms spread liberally among the faithful, in ordinary acts of love performed in Christ's name, in the witness of the great saints, in the inspired art, poetry, and architecture of the Catholic tradition, etc. This manifold display prevents the holiness of the Church from becoming a mere abstraction or velleity. It can be seen and touched and verified.

The English word "holy" is related, of course, to the word "whole," and indeed, in a variety of other languages, holiness and "wholeness" or good health are closely linked. Thus, *sanctus* and *sanus* in Latin, *saint* and *sain* in French, *santo* and *sano* in Spanish, etc. Therefore, holiness carries the sense of well-being and integration. We might bring these two senses of the term together in this context as follows: the Church is that community that, having been set apart, participates in the distinctiveness and transcendence of God and thereby brings fullness of life to its members.

In regard to this mark of the Church, we confront, once again, a serious objection. How could the Church be described as holy when so many of its adepts have done so many terrible things, often in its name? How could the Church that sponsored the Inquisition, witch hunts, persecution of dissidents, the harassing of Galileo, and the execution of Giordano Bruno possibly be holy? How could the Church that has accumulated massive wealth and been marked, up and down the centuries, by extraordinary institutional corruption and has, in recent years, been guilty of countenancing the crime of the sexual abuse of children possibly be a source of healing and integration? In study after study, the rather manifest unholiness of the Church is cited as a key reason for disaffiliation from Catholicism, especially on the part of young people.

But a distinction is in order. Every single person up and down the centuries who has ever been a member of the Church (with the exception of the Blessed Mother) has been a sinner. Even the greatest of the saints were sinners—and they would be the first to tell you as much, for precisely those who are navigating their lives in the direction of the light are most likely to see smudges and imperfections on the windowpane of their souls. Every single officeholder in the history of the Church has been a sinner and thus altogether likely to abuse his power. In point of fact, the doctrine of original sin, which teaches that all of us are members of a dysfunctional family, predisposes us to expect some degree of failure, corruption, stupidity, cruelty, and injustice on the part of everyone at every level. But none of this tells against the holiness of the Church, which is not dependent upon the vibrant sanctity and moral excellence of the baptized, but rather upon the Holy Spirit and those clear manifestations of the Spirit's influence referenced above.

The distinction upon which I am insisting here was the fulcrum on which St. Augustine's resolution of the Donatist controversy turned. The followers of Donatus, an African bishop of the early fourth century, claimed that priests who had apostatized during a time of persecution and who then sought to return to active ministry after the danger had passed could not administer valid sacraments. Against this, Augustine raised his voice in strenuous protest, for the Donatist position seemed to give to sin the power to negate the objective efficacy of the Holy Spirit. To be sure, Augustine was really only giving more specific definition to St. Paul's observation in his Second Letter to the Corinthians that the Church holds the treasure of Christ in exceptionally fragile vessels (2 Cor. 4:7). The corruption of the containers should not negate the reality of the treasure.

Catholic

The third principal mark of the Church, according to the Creed, is catholicity. The term "catholic" is derived from the Greek *kata holos* (according to the whole) and thus designates something like universal or all-embracing. As such, this ecclesial mark is closely tied to that of unity. Since God wants to draw all people to himself, his outreach is properly all-englobing and so must be the vehicle by which he effects this gathering-in. Accordingly, the Church of Jesus Christ cannot be limited to any one nation, any single region, any particular ethnic group, or the speakers of any one language exclusively. Such a limitation would be repugnant to the catholic trajectory and purpose of the Church. St. Paul saw this with extraordinary clarity within a few years of the founding: "As many of you as were baptized into Christ have clothed yourselves with Christ. There is no longer Jew or Greek, there is no longer slave or free, there is no longer male or female; for all of you are one in Christ Jesus" (Gal. 3:27–28). Paul is choosing here, provocatively enough, some of the most significant fault lines in the society of his time. To know one's religion, ethnicity, social standing, and gender was practically tantamount to knowing who one was. Therefore, blithely to say that none of these finally matters and that an identity more fundamental has emerged was to start a social revolution. That Paul spent a good deal of time in jail proves it.

What put an end to the animosity based on cultural, ethnic, and religious differences was, of course, the cross of Jesus, which represented God's swallowing up of any and all human dysfunction. Paul expressed this idea with unsurpassed clarity in his Letter to the Ephesians. Addressing a contentious Jewish and Gentile community, he says: "But now in Christ Jesus you who once were far off have been brought near by the blood of Christ. For he is our peace; in his flesh he has made both groups into one and has broken down the dividing wall, that is, the hostility between us" (Eph. 2:13–14). Hence, the cross of Christ is the matrix of catholicity, the means by which God overcame the divisions of the fallen world. Once again, this ought to relieve the concerns of those who might see in the catholicizing push toward universality a disguised power play. The only legitimate imperialism within the Church is the imperialism of the one crowned with thorns and reigning from a Roman cross.

In all of this we should see something of great practical and pastoral moment—namely, that the Church is not simply a community that in principle welcomes people from all nations, races, ethnic groups, educational backgrounds, etc.; it is most especially the place where the tensions produced by these divisions are actively overcome. The Church is an agent and instrument of reconciliation, within itself and outside of itself. And this is why whenever the Church has contributed to division, ethnic violence, racial prejudice, or intercultural animosity, it is operating in a manner utterly repugnant to its own nature.

Still another dimension of the Church's catholicity is this: it has, in the words of Cardinal Francis George, "all the gifts Christ wants to give us." There is not only a "here comes everybody" quality about the Catholic Church, but also a "here is everything" quality as well, for it includes Scripture, the liturgy, a richly complex theological tradition, the sacraments, the Eucharistic presence, Mary and the saints, the apostolic succession of the bishops, papal authority, mysticism, a deep commitment to social justice, etc. The *kata holos* principle powerfully holds sway with respect to the inner life of the Church. A mentor of mine once commented that part of the genius of Catholicism is that "we never threw anything away." In the great storehouse of the Church, the full wealth of Christ can be found.

Mind you, none of this implies that other Christian denominations and indeed other religions might not represent some of these qualities better or more fully than the Catholic Church does. For instance, some Protestant communions have a more developed sense of the centrality of the Bible and preaching, and the Orthodox Church might have a more impressively mystical appreciation of the liturgy. But none of them possess the full range of the gifts, the catholic totality.

Perhaps just a word as I draw this section on catholicity to a close regarding a standard objection. Some have maintained that the term "Roman Catholic" is simply incoherent, for the first word designates a very particular place while the second word indicates the *universum*. The one thing, it appears, a Roman church cannot be is catholic. The resolution of this dilemma depends upon the biblical principle articulated earlier, that individuals are always chosen not for themselves but for the world. Israel was indeed the uniquely elect people, but they were elected for the sake of mission. The Church is Roman precisely because Peter was chosen by Christ to be the bearer of the keys and he died as leader of the Christian community in Rome. But Peter (and hence Rome) was chosen for the world, not for his own sake. This creative tension is beautifully expressed in the Bernini colonnade that reaches out, just like two arms, from St. Peter's Basilica in Rome, in a gesture of universal embrace.

And apostolic Church

And this observation segues neatly into the fourth and final mark of the Church referenced by the Nicene Creed: apostolicity. The one, holy, and catholic Church is grounded in the small band of twelve men whom Jesus called to himself and shaped according to his own mind and heart. At the root of all of the institutional structure and world-spanning reach of the Church is, finally, this intimate company of Jesus, gathered as apprentices around a master. Once again, this apostolic principle shows that Christianity is not an abstract philosophical system or a spirituality flowing from personal experience; it is a relationship to the very particular Christ, whose first preachers and mediators were the Twelve. When the two disciples of John the Baptist followed after Jesus, the Master turned and asked them, "What are you looking for?" The startled response came: "Where are you staying?" And Jesus said, "Come and see" (John 1:38–39). The Church takes its origins and finds its orientation from the first companions who came and saw, who stayed where the Lord stayed.

But to characterize the Church as apostolic is not simply to make a statement regarding its history and etiology. The apostolicity of the *ekklesia* is evident in what we call the "apostolic succession"—which is to say, the passing on of the Apostles' authority from one generation to the next in the persons of bishops. Through the laying on of hands, bishops across time and space have received, as a charism of the Holy Spirit, the mission and identity of apostles. They have been invited, so to speak, into the same relationship of special intimacy with Christ that was enjoyed by Peter, Matthew, John, Thomas, and the others.

It is through the bishops, therefore, that the integrity of the Church's teaching, worship, and pastoral service is guaranteed. This means that those intimately bound to Jesus assure that the Church is not simply teaching according to the evanescent philosophy of a given age, or worshiping a God other than the one Jesus called "Father," or serving the poor out of purely secular motivation or with a purely political purpose. This of course does not mean that the bishops directly perform all of these tasks at the highest level. Thomas Aquinas was a greater theologian than any bishop of his time; Mother Teresa served the poor more effectively and dramatically than any bishop of her time. But it does mean that the successors of the Apostles play a refereeing and supervisory role vis-à-vis all such work in the Church.

I confess one Baptism for the forgiveness of sins

As a coda to this treatment of the Church, the Creed adds, "I confess one Baptism for the forgiveness of sins." We notice the shift from belief to confession, for we are professing here not a core point of doctrine, but rather a practice of the Church, though admittedly one so central that it is the only practice referenced in the Creed. One reason, of course, that Baptism comes in for special treatment is that the Nicene declaration, like the earlier Apostles' Creed, grew up out of confessions made by the faithful in advance of their reception into the Church. "Do you believe in God? Do you believe in Jesus Christ? Do you believe in the Holy Spirit?" etc.

However, there is a deeper reason for its prominence, for Baptism is the *sine qua non* of the Christian life, what the Council of Florence called the *vitae spiritualis ianua* (the door of the spiritual life), that without which none of the doctrines articulated in the Creed would make, finally, any existential difference in the life of a person. By Baptism, one is configured to Christ in such a way that one begins to share the relationship between the Father and the Son. And as we saw when examining the Trinitarian relations, this implies a real participation in the Holy Spirit, who *is* the love between the Father and the Son. Thus, this originating sacrament, which is always performed "in the name of the Father, and of the Son, and of the Holy Spirit," is the means by which an initiate commences to share in the inner dynamics of the Trinity, which is the entire point of the spiritual life. Everything else in Christian existence—reading of Scripture, participation in the liturgy, the study of theology, service of the poor, evangelization, the reception of the other sacraments—comes from this or returns to it.

The Creed names as the effect of Baptism "the forgiveness of sins," and indeed this cleansing is a major consequence of the sacrament. We might parse this relationship as follows. When we are drawn into the inner dynamics of the Trinitarian life, we are taken up into an altogether new manner of existence. Since the divine life *is* love, sin is repugnant to it, and hence God's gracious inclusion of someone into the play of the Trinitarian persons must be accompanied by the erasure of sin. We might also say that Baptism entails the forgiveness of sins in the measure that it brings us into the life of the

Church—and hence calls us out of the fallen world and into something altogether new.

6

The World to Come

And I look forward to the resurrection of the dead

DEATH HAUNTS THE WHOLE OF OUR LIFE here below. Its inevitability and finality cast a shadow over even the greatest of our achievements and the most intense of our pleasures. Because, at the end of the day, we will die, it can easily appear to us that human life, ultimately, is pointless. Indeed, contemporary cosmologists and astrophysicists have only intensified this sense of meaninglessness by reminding us that the earth will one day be swallowed up by the sun, the sun will eventually burn out, and the universe itself is destined finally to pass into the virtual nonexistence of total entropy. The physical universe is marked by both order and chaos, but there seems little doubt that the latter triumphs, at last, over the former.

But we who have professed our faith in God, maker of heaven and earth, cannot resign ourselves to this cosmic futility. If God has made the entire universe, then he cannot leave it simply to wink out of existence. And he most certainly cannot abandon to oblivion his human creatures, who long for him with all their hearts, whether they know it or not. One of the most impressive Old Testament witnesses to this truth is found in the second book of Maccabees. We read that a pious Israelite mother and her seven sons have been arrested for refusing to eat pork during the time of the persecution of Antiochus IV. One by one, the sons are tortured to death in the most horrific manner and in the presence of their mother. As he is dying, the second son says to his torturers, "You dismiss us from this present life, but the King of the universe will raise us up to an everlasting renewal of life" (2 Macc. 7:9). And the third son, when it is asked of him, willingly puts out his tongue and his hands, and says, "I got these from Heaven, and because of his laws I disdain them, and from him I hope to get them back again" (2 Macc. 7:11). This grisly but wonderful passage shows not only the emergence of a belief in life after death among Old Testament Jews, but also how that belief is tied to a keen sense of God's goodness and justice. As we saw earlier, if the righteous who are not vindicated in this world find no vindication in a life to come, then the Lord is not just.

Jesus himself professed the truth of the resurrection when he commented that the God of Abraham, Isaac, and Jacob—three figures long dead—is nevertheless not the God of the dead but of the living. For those who believe in the Creator God, protology (the beginning of things) implies eschatology (the consummation of things). And therefore, we "look forward" to our own resurrection and the life of the world to come. The language of the Creed correctly implies that we do not have anything like an exhaustive knowledge of the state of affairs that will obtain after our deaths or at the end of the spatiotemporal universe. But we look, we wait, we hope.

What precisely does "resurrection of the dead" mean? I will not repeat all that I said just a few chapters ago in regard to Jesus' Resurrection; suffice it to say that this hope is not focused on a Platonic escape of the soul from the body, but rather, as the Maccabees passage shows so vividly, on the renovation, transfiguration, and restoration of the whole person. It strikes biblically minded people as foolish to hold that the God who made the body and the material world would simply give up on all of that as a lost cause and rescue a spiritual element from it. Whatever else final salvation involves, it is, most certainly, a bodily state of affairs. But how do we make sense of this? In the face of death, burial, and decomposition, does not this talk of eternal life and resurrection just seem impossibly far-fetched? Are the critics of Christianity not correct in seeing this as the crudest kind of wish-fulfilling fantasy? The Church does not claim for an instant that it has worked out the details of the transition to eternal life, but it has entertained certain models by which the language of resurrection might be understood.

I realize that, even as I indulged in it a moment ago, the setting up of Plato as a foil is more than a tad facile. The dualism of Plato, which certainly from a scriptural standpoint is finally untenable, nevertheless reveals a rather profound truth about human beings. And Platonic-style thinking to a degree helps us to pick our way through some thorny intellectual ground as we struggle to make sense of what our biblical faith is compelling us to say. The doctrine of the Church is that those who have died, and whose earthly bodies have decayed, will rise bodily on the last day. Therefore, there has to be some continuity between the life that has rather obviously ended here below and the life to come. It is in trying to puzzle this out that the Church has turned to the language of soul and immortality, and Plato has proven to be an important intellectual ally in this respect.

Plato clearly saw that the human mind is capable of considering mathematical truths and pure abstract forms, which by definition stand outside of the realm of passing, contingent things. Therefore, the mind, at least in its higher functions, cannot be reduced to the operations of a material organ such as the brain. Thus, we have Plato's great teacher, Socrates, within moments of his death, calmly explaining to his grieving disciples that his soul will live on in the realm of the forms. Now, Plato's student Aristotle, uneasy with the stark dualism of his master's anthropology, opined that the soul is best understood as the "form" or fundamental animating pattern of the body. This helped to solve the problem of dualism, but it also made the soul essentially as evanescent as the body.

One of the most extraordinary intellectual accomplishments of Thomas Aquinas was to have effected a hybrid of Platonic and Aristotelian anthropology in regard to the soul. In line with Aristotle, Thomas held that *anima* (soul) is best construed as *forma corporis* (the form of the body), and this he did not simply out of devotion to Aristotle but because of his biblical commitments. No reader of the opening chapters of Genesis could ever think that the material body is properly understood as a prison for the soul. That sort of antagonistic dualism is simply repugnant to the Scriptures, which teach that God found everything that he had made very good. At the same time, again for biblical reasons, Thomas knew that the Aristotelian soul, in the measure that it would evanesce with the dissolution of the body, is irreconcilable with the hope for eternal life. Thus, he argued that, remaining the form of the body, the *anima* has a subsistent quality, precisely inasmuch as it possesses the capacity to engage in acts of pure intellection.

By means of the senses, the soul can take in the outside world, and through memory and imagination, it can form pictorial representations of that world, but by the intellect, it can abstract formal patterns from particular sense data and images. Thus, commencing with mental pictures of individual human beings, the mind is capable of distilling and holding the form of humanity—which is to say, the essential pattern that all human beings have in common. Or from seven particular things, the intellect can abstract the sheer idea of the number seven. In both of these cases, the mind is dealing with a reality that cannot be material, since it has to be equally valid of any and all individual instances of either humanity or sevenness. If intellectual activity were simply reducible to brain function, this sort of move would be ruled out, for all that a material organ could possibly manage is the processing of sense data and/or images. This proved to Aquinas' satisfaction that the soul, at least in its higher functions, is immaterial and hence does not disintegrate with the death of the body.

Hence, we can and should speak of disincarnate souls that live on after death, but keeping the Aristotelianism of Aquinas in mind, we should also insist that those disembodied souls retain an orientation to the flesh. In their purely spiritual manner of existence, they have not found the rest they finally seek. What they long for is precisely what the Creed calls "the resurrection of the dead"—namely, their reintegration with materiality—and this will take place at the end of time, or outside of time. The Platonic element within Thomas' treatment provides for the needed continuity between this life and the resurrected life. Ultimately, it is not the literally self-same matter that guarantees the identity of one's earthly body and one's heavenly body, but rather the enduring sameness of one's soul.

Out of what materials does God make the resurrected body? Could an elevated body—both like and unlike the body here below—be what St. Paul refers to, with intentional ambiguity, as a "spiritual body"? To be sure, all of this is highly speculative, and no Christian is obliged to accept in every detail any particular theory. We really do not know the mechanics behind the transformation involved in the resurrection of the flesh. What the Creed demands that we "look forward to" is an embodied life on high with God, which is both a continuation of the life we live here below and something so new that of it we are compelled to say with St. Paul, "No eye has seen, nor ear heard, nor the human heart conceived, what God has prepared for those who love him" (1 Cor. 2:9).

And the life of the world to come

Nevertheless, theologians and spiritual writers have proposed models or images to describe "the life of the world to come." One of the most fundamental metaphors for the life of heaven is the beatific vision—the awareness, the consciousness, that makes us finally happy. The matrix out of which this comparison comes is intellectual, the "seeing" involved in acts of knowing. The mind seeks the truth and frequently finds it, but every finding opens up a plethora of new questions. And thus the mind moves ever onward, upward, inward, in a relentless quest to see.

Inspired by his Thomistic heritage, Bernard Lonergan said that what the restless mind ultimately wants is "to know everything about everything." This all-inclusive seeing—obviously impossible to us in this life—*is* the beatific vision, which will represent the culmination of intellectual actualization in the world to come. It is tantamount to knowing the very essence of God, the source of all being and truth, or to put it in more scriptural terms, to seeing God face to face. But how, we might ask, would this knowledge of God ever be possible, even in heaven, to a finite mind? Thomas Aquinas answers that it happens only through a graced and supernatural elevation of the intellect, the gift of participating in God's manner of knowing himself. But even having said that, we must add that, for Aquinas, this could never, even for the elevated mind, amount to total comprehension, but only to the joy of unending exploration into God.

In seeing God face to face, we shall also thereby see all those beings and events that participate in God. Dante expresses this toward the end of the *Paradiso*, using the image of a book. St. Bernard invites Dante to look into the loveliness of God, and Dante says, "I saw how it contains within its depths / all things bound in a single book by love / of which creation is the scattered leaves." In a word, we will see, in God, the great work of art, only hints of which we can possibly spy in this life.

A second model for understanding the nature of heaven is that of a city. The Bible is replete with bucolic imagery—think of the "green pastures" to which the good shepherd will lead us (Ps. 23:2)—and it remains rather suspicious of cities. Think of Cain as the founder of cities and all of the kingdoms of the world belonging to Satan.

But when speaking of the consummation of things, the Scriptures utilize an urban image.

At the conclusion of the book of Revelation, we read of the arrival of the new heavens and the new earth, and then of "the holy city, the new Jerusalem, coming down out of heaven from God, prepared as a bride adorned for her husband" (Rev. 21:2). The metaphor of vision, as rich as it is, might give the impression that the life of heaven is a solitary, contemplative affair, but to say that heaven is like a city is to signal something else altogether. Cities are places where enormous crowds of people come together for business, for entertainment, for sports, for leisure activity, for the arts, for communication, and for communal living. They are loud, bustling, energetic, full of excitement and rich possibility. To be sure, here below, they are also places of loneliness, exclusion, and violence, but because anything of the sinful is removed from heaven, the city on high retains the beauty of life in intense communion with none of the dross.

Will there be sports, entertainment, creative arts, and business in the heavenly realm? I do not see how people in that city could be truly happy without them, again keeping in mind that such activities will produce neither conflict nor boredom. Mind you, the author of the book of Revelation is keen to communicate to us, above all, the *beauty* of the new Jerusalem: "The wall is built of jasper, while the city is pure gold, clear as glass. The foundations of the wall of the city are adorned with every jewel" (Rev. 21:18–19). We should not interpret this as mere decoration, but rather as an indication that all the activity of the heavenly city is marked by wholeness, harmony, and radiance.

Just after the lengthy description of the new Jerusalem's beauty, we find this extraordinary assertion: "I saw no temple in the city, for its temple is the Lord God the Almighty and the Lamb. And the city has no need of sun or moon to shine on it, for the glory of God is its light" (Rev. 21:22–23). For any Jew of the first century, the temple was the center, the very *raison d'être*, of Jerusalem. Whatever else happened in that capital city was related to the temple and its rituals, and God was seen as, in a practically literal sense, dwelling within the walls of that holy place. If all the tribes of the world came to Jerusalem, it was because of the temple. Therefore, what sense does it make to say that the perfected Jerusalem has no temple?

There is no formal religious edifice in the heavenly city *because the entire city has become a place of right praise*. In our fallen world, temples and churches are vivid reminders to bring our lives, public and private, into alignment with God. As Paul Tillich taught, the very presence of these buildings is hence an indication of the sinfulness of the world. In a rightly ordered society, play, sports, business, finance, family life, and politics are all effortlessly ordered to the worship of God—and hence no temple is needed. Notice that the author of Revelation says that the glory of God is the light of the new city, which would seem to indicate that every activity takes place through divine illumination and for a divinely ordained end.

This connection helps us then to understand a final great image for heaven—namely, the eternal liturgy. I know from a good deal of pastoral experience that this comparison can leave many people uninspired, given the blandness and banality of too many liturgies here below.

But we must recall that right praise is perhaps the central theme of the entire Bible, for sin is the falling away from "orthodoxy," and salvation is its restoration. Putting God in the center, making God the highest value, is the essential prerequisite of a properly ordered spiritual and moral life. Hence, what we see in the joyful bustle of the heavenly Jerusalem, that city without a temple, is precisely the effect of right praise.

We should not think of heaven as an endless version of liturgy on earth, but rather we should see liturgy here below as a vague indication of the orthodoxy that constitutes the life of heaven. In the new Jerusalem, we shall live in community, sing in harmony, understand the divine truth, commune with the angels, internalize the body and blood of Christ, converse face to face with God, and enter ever more deeply into a life of love. Take away from our worship on earth all that smacks of boredom, resentment, or incomprehension, and take all that awakens a deeper communion with the Trinitarian God, and we might have some sense of what God has prepared for those who love him.

Notes

1. I Believe

3 it does so out of love: Thomas Aquinas, *Summa theologiae* 2-2.2.

4 how we make our way into or toward the mystery of God: Bonaventure, *The Soul's Journey into God*, in *Bonaventure: The Soul's Journey into God, The Tree of Life, and The Life of St. Francis*, trans. Ewert Cousins (Mahwah, NJ: Paulist, 1978), 51–116.

5 the exercise of our rational faculties: First Vatican Council, *Dei Filius* 2, in Heinrich Denzinger et al., *Compendium of Creeds, Definitions, and Declarations on Matters of Faith and Morals*, 43rd ed. (San Francisco: Ignatius, 2012), nos. 3000–3007.

5 *viae* or "paths" to God: Thomas Aquinas, *Summa theologiae* 1.2.3 (Leon. 4:31–32).

5 "leadings by the hand": Thomas Aquinas, *Summa theologiae* 1.1.5 ad 2 (Leon. 4:16).

5 the warrant of the physical sciences: See Robert Barron, *Arguing Religion: A Bishop Speaks at Facebook and Google* (Park Ridge, IL: Word on Fire, 2018), 17–26; Robert Barron and John L. Allen Jr., *To Light a Fire on the Earth* (New York: Image Books, 2017), 103–105; and Robert Barron, *Renewing Our Hope: Essays for the New Evangelization* (Washington, DC: The Catholic University of America Press, 2020), 12–18.

7 "it is something that the mathematicians can recognize and agree about": John Polkinghorne, "The Trinity and Scientific Reality," in *The Blackwell Companion to Science and Christianity,* ed. J.B. Stump and Alan G. Padgett (Oxford: Wiley-Blackwell, 2012), 524.

7 **Where do the laws of nature come from:** See Paul Davies, "The Nature of the Laws of Physics and Their Mysterious Bio-Friendliness," in *Science and Religion in Dialogue*, vol. 2, ed. Melville Y. Stewart (Oxford: Wiley-Blackwell, 2010), 769–788.

7 **"The most incomprehensible thing about the universe is that it is comprehensible":** Albert Einstein, "Physics and Reality," *Journal of the Franklin Institute* 221, no. 3 (March 1936): 351.

8 **the structure of the universe:** Joseph Ratzinger, *Introduction to Christianity*, 2nd ed., trans. J.R. Foster (San Francisco: Ignatius, 2004), 151–158.

10 **to take a stand—both for and against:** Ratzinger, *Introduction to Christianity*, 110–115.

10 *actus purus* **in the language of Thomas Aquinas:** Thomas Aquinas, *Summa theologiae* 1.9.1 (Leon. 4.90–91).

11 **"there are more beings but not more perfection of** *esse* **[being]":** Robert Sokolowski, *The God of Faith and Reason: Foundations of Christian Theology* (Washington, DC: The Catholic University of America Press, 1995), 42.

2. The Father

13 **the good is diffusive of itself:** See, for example, Pseudo-Dionysius, *The Divine Names* 4, in *Pseudo-Dionysius: The Complete Works*, trans. Colm Luibheid (New York: Paulist, 1987), 71–96. For the phrase *bonum diffusivum sui*, see Thomas Aquinas' discussions of Dionysius' principle in *Summa theologiae* 1.5.4, 1.27.5, 1.73.3, 1-2.1.4, and elsewhere.

13 **to will the good of the other:** Thomas Aquinas, *Summa theologiae* 1-2.26.4 co.; *Summa contra Gentiles* 1.91.2–3, trans. Anton C. Pegis (New York: Hanover House, 1955). See also *Catechism of the Catholic Church* 1766.

13 **"Our praises add nothing to your greatness":** "Common Preface IV," in *Roman Missal* (ICEL, 2010).

15 **a kind of relation to God with newness of being:** Thomas Aquinas, *Quaestiones disputatae de potentia Dei* 3.3, in *Quaestiones disputatae*, vol. 2, ed. P. Bazzi (Turin: Marietti, 1949) (my translation).

15 **God sustains the universe the way a singer sustains a song:** Herbert McCabe, *God Still Matters*, ed. Brian Davies (New York: Continuum, 2005), 234.

15 **you are here and now being created by God:** See Thomas Merton, *New Seeds of Contemplation* (New York: New Directions, 1961), 1–5.

16 **God is also closer to us than we are to ourselves:** See Augustine, *Confessions*, trans. F.J. Sheed, ed. Michael P. Foley (Park Ridge, IL: Word on Fire Classics, 2017), 50.

18 **the lack of a good that ought to be present:** Augustine, *Confessions*, 139–167.

20 **Heidegger recovered the primordial understanding of truth as visibility or coming into the light:** Martin Heidegger, *Being and Truth*, trans. Gregory Fried and Richard Polt (Bloomington, IN: Indiana University Press, 2010), 110–152.

20 **Thomas Aquinas states that all knowledge begins in the senses:** See, for example, Thomas Aquinas, *Questiones disputatae de veritate* 1.11, trans. Robert W. Mulligan, SJ (Chicago: Henry Regnery, 1952).

20 **a more substantial, though invisible, world of pure forms:** Plato, *Republic* 514a–520a, trans. C.D.C. Reeve (Indianapolis, IN: Hackett, 2004), 208–214.

22 **whether there are forms of ordinary and crass things, such as mud and hair:** Plato, *Parmenides* 130b–c, trans. Mary Louise Gill and Paul Ryan (Indianapolis, IN: Hackett, 1996), 130–131.

3. The Son

24 sin is turning from God to creatures: Augustine, *Confessions*, trans. F.J. Sheed, ed. Michael P. Foley (Park Ridge, IL: Word on Fire Classics, 2017), 24–25.

31 Jesus' bearing and overall manner of life make these explanations completely unconvincing: C.S. Lewis, *Mere Christianity* (New York: HarperOne, 2009), 47–52. See also Peter Kreeft and Ronald Tacelli, *Handbook of Catholic Apologetics: Reasoned Answers to Questions of Faith* (San Francisco: Ignatius, 2009), 166–183.

32 "There was a time when he was not": Quoted in Alexander of Alexandria, *Deposition of Arius* 2.2, trans. Miles Atkinson and Archibald T. Robertson, in Nicene and Post-Nicene Fathers, Second Series, vol. 4, ed. Philip Schaff and Henry Wace (Buffalo, NY: Christian Literature, 1892), 70.

34 the bishop of Alexandria clarified the subtle distinction between begetting and making: Athanasius, *Four Discourses Against the Arians*, trans. John Henry Newman and Archibald Robertson, in NPNF² 4, ed. Philip Schaff and Henry Wace (Buffalo, NY: Christian Literature, 1892), 306–447.

38 the dilemma bequeathed to the Church by the Nicene Creed and that, sixteen centuries later, still beguiles and illumines: Augustine, *De trinitate* 9. For a recent English translation of this work, see *The Trinity*, trans. Edmund Hill, ed. John E. Rotelle, in *The Works of Saint Augustine: A Translation for the 21st Century*, vol. 5 (New York: New City, 1990).

42 "ultimate concern": Paul Tillich, *Systematic Theology* (Chicago: University of Chicago Press, 1967), 8–12, 211–213.

46 only superficially similar: Hans Urs von Balthasar, *Credo: Meditations on the Apostles' Creed*, trans. David Kipp (San Francisco: Ignatius, 2005), 47–48.

49 "without confusion or change, without division or separation": Council of Chalcedon, the Chalcedonian Creed, in Heinrich Denzinger et al., *Compendium of Creeds, Definitions, and Declarations on Matters of Faith and Morals*, 43rd ed. (San Francisco: Ignatius, 2012), nos. 302, 109.

52 "that than which nothing greater can be thought": Anselm, *Proslogion* 2–5, in *Anselm: Monologion and Proslogion*, trans. Thomas Williams (Indianapolis, IN: Hackett, 1996), 99–102.

52 "God became man that man might become God": See, for example, Athanasius, *De incarnatione* 54 (PG 25:192). For an English translation of this work, see *On the Incarnation*, trans. John Behr (Yonkers, NY: St. Vladimir's Seminary, 2011).

56 the darkness of the world is made fully manifest: Karl Barth, *Church Dogmatics*, 4.1, *The Doctrine of Reconciliation* (Edinburgh: T&T Clark, 1988), 358–477.

57 the ever-increasing *agon* between Jesus and the world that he enters: John Courtney Murray, *An Eight Day Retreat*, unpublished manuscript.

57 he had to sneak clandestinely behind enemy lines: Lewis, *Mere Christianity*, 45–46.

57 the shock of the cross: See Søren Kierkegaard, *Concluding Unscientific Postscript to Philosophical Fragments*, vol. 1, ed. and trans. Howard V. Hong and Edna H. Hong (Princeton, NJ: Princeton University Press, 1992).

57 a peculiar remark: Fleming Rutledge, *The Crucifixion: Understanding the Death of Jesus Christ* (Grand Rapids, MI: Eerdmans, 2015), 1–4.

60 the emergence of Christianity as a *messianic* movement is, to say the very least, an anomaly: N.T. Wright, *Surprised by Scripture* (New York: HarperOne, 2014), 49–52.

61 the *Christus Victor* theory: Gustaf Aulén, *Christus Victor: An Historical Study of the Three Main Types of the Idea of Atonement*, trans. A.G. Herbert (Eugene, OR: Wipf & Stock, 2003).

65 that a price be paid to restore that honor: Anselm, *Why God Became Man* 1.11, in *Anselm of Canterbury: The Major Works,* ed. Brian Davies and G.R. Evans (New York: Oxford World's Classics, 2008), 282–284.

66 only by the suffering and death of someone who is both God and man: Anselm, *Why God Became Man* 2.6, 319–320.

66 its principal virtue is that it takes the real damage of sin seriously: Anselm, *Cur Deus homo* 21 (PL 158:393–394), *Why God Became Man*, 305–306.

66 it would not have *repaired* what needed repairing: Thomas Aquinas, *Summa theologiae* 3.1.2.

66 the furthest trajectory of the Incarnation: Hans Urs von Balthasar, *Mysterium Paschale*, trans. Aidan Nichols (San Francisco: Ignatius, 2000).

68 the "being dead" of God: Balthasar, *Mysterium Paschale*, 168–188.

69 "A great silence because the King is asleep": *Catechism of the Catholic Church* 635.

69 "Why, a man's faith might be ruined by looking at that picture!": Fyodor Dostoevsky, *The Idiot*, trans. Eva M. Martin (Overland Park, KS: Digireads, 2018), 172.

72 the purpose of Christian theology is to make Christianity *hard* to believe: See, for example, Kierkegaard, *Concluding Unscientific Postscript to Philosophical Fragments*, 186–187.

72 delineating, first, how it should not be understood: N.T. Wright, *The Resurrection of the Son of God* (Minneapolis, MN: Fortress, 2003), 1–206.

79 revelations of the true laws of nature, of nature as it is intended to be: Flannery O'Connor, *The Habit of Being: Letters of Flannery O'Connor* (New York: Farrar, Straus & Giroux, 1979), 100. Quoted in *Flannery O'Connor Collection*, ed. Matthew Becklo (Park Ridge, IL: Word on Fire Classics, 2019), 64–65.

86 "Hosanna in the highest": "Preface III of the Sundays in Ordinary Time" and "Preface Acclamation," in *Roman Missal* (ICEL, 2010).

87 "axle around which the whole country blindly turns": Thomas Merton, *Run to the Mountain: The Story of a Vocation*, ed. Patrick Hart (San Francisco: Harper, 1995), 333.

4. The Holy Spirit

94 the *Spiritus Sanctus*, the Holy Breath: Fulton J. Sheen, *The Divine Romance: Falling in Love with God* (Chicago: Biretta Books, 2014), 15–16.

98 their shared willing is the purest love possible, the very essence of love: See Robert Barron, "The One Who Is, the One Who Gives: Derrida, Aquinas, and the Dilemma of Divine Generosity," in *Renewing Our Hope: Essays for the New Evangelization* (Washington, DC: The Catholic University of America Press, 2020), 97–112.

100 so we have something to say when people ask us what they are: See Augustine, *On the Trinity* 5.2.9–10, 7.3.8–9, ed. John Rotelle, trans. Edmund Hill (Hyde Park, NY: New City, 1991), 197, 229–230.

100 three I don't know whats: Anselm, *Monologion* 78 (PL 158:221–222).

101 Aquinas referred to the Trinitarian persons as "subsistent relations": Thomas Aquinas, *Summa theologiae* 1.29.4, 1.40.2.

106 to evaluate the affairs of the world from the perspective of God and God's purposes: Yves Congar, *True and False Reform in the Church*, trans. Paul Philibert (Collegeville, MN: Liturgical, 2011), 136.

106 **the prophet is someone who feels the feelings of God and then speaks out of that experience:** Abraham Joshua Heschel, *The Prophets* (New York: Harper Perennial Classics, 2001).

107 **"he reverses the apparent order of things that is actually false, and rediscovers the real order":** André Rousseaux, *Le prophète Péguy*, vol. 1 (Neuchâtel, CH: La Baconnière, 1945), 119. Quoted in Yves Congar, *True and False Reform in the Church*, 138.

107 **Christ's fool actually sees things aright:** G.K. Chesterton, *Orthodoxy* (Park Ridge, IL: Word on Fire Classics, 2017), 161–163.

5. The Church

110 **"Christ made His brothers, called together from all nations, mystically the components of His own Body":** *Lumen Gentium* 7, in *The Word on Fire Vatican II Collection*, ed. Matthew Levering (Park Ridge, IL: Word on Fire Institute, 2021), 51.

111 **"through such outward approaches as I shall assign":** John Henry Newman, *Lectures on the Doctrine of Justification* (London: Longmans & Green, 1908), 216–217.

112 **What Charles Williams called co-inherence applies par excellence to the life of the Church:** Charles Williams, *Charles Williams: Essential Writings in Theology and Spirituality*, ed. Charles Hefling (Cambridge: Cowley, 1993), 17–18.

112 **"How [these Christians] love one another!":** Tertullian, *Apology* 39.7, trans. T.R. Glover, Loeb Classical Library (London: William Heinemann, 1931), 177.

112 **"I simply know they're just one thing, and we shouldn't complicate the matter":** *Acts of the Trial of Joan of Arc*, quoted in *Catechism of the Catholic Church* 795.

116 **the Church *is* a mission, by its very nature:** Pope Paul VI,

Evangelii Nuntiandi 14–15, apostolic exhortation, December 8, 1975, vatican.va

116 a symbol of ecclesial introversion: Pope Francis, "Chrism Mass: Homily of Pope Francis," March 28, 2013, vatican.va.

122 the fulcrum on which St. Augustine's resolution of the Do-natist controversy turned: Augustine, *The Writings Against the Man-ichaeans and Against the Donatists*, NPNF[1] 4, ed. Philip Schaff (Buffalo, NY: Christian Literature, 1887).

124 "all the gifts Christ wants to give us": Francis George, *A Godly Humanism: Clarifying the Hope That Lies Within* (Washington, DC: The Catholic University of America Press, 2015), 93.

128 the door of the spiritual life: Council of Florence, quoted in *Cat-echism of the Catholic Church* 1213.

6. The World to Come

133 his soul will live on in the realm of the forms: Plato, *Phaedo*, trans. David Gallop (Oxford: Oxford World's Classics, 2009).

133 the soul is best understood as the "form" or fundamental ani-mating pattern of the body: Aristotle, *De anima*, trans. C.D.C. Reeve (Indianapolis, IN: Hackett, 2017).

133 not simply out of devotion to Aristotle but because of his bib-lical commitments: Thomas Aquinas, *Summa theologiae* 1.76.1 (Leon. 5:208–209); *Summa contra Gentiles* 2.68–72 (Leon. 13:198–213), trans. James Anderson (New York: Hanover House, 1955).

134 the capacity to engage in acts of pure intellection: Thomas Aquinas, *Summa contra Gentiles* 2.79–80.

136 "to know everything about everything": Bernard Lonergan, *In-sight: A Study of Human Understanding* (New York: Philosophical Li-brary, 1958), 350–351.

136 **"creation is the scattered leaves":** Dante Alighieri, *The Divine Comedy*, vol. 3, *Paradise*, trans. Mark Musa (New York: Penguin Books, 1986), canto 33.392.